Diary of a

MODERN COUNTRY GARDENER

Secrets for every season,
straight from the potting shed.

Tamsin Westhorpe

with illustrations by
Hannah Madden and Rosalie Herrera

ORPHANS
publishing

About the Author

Tamsin is a hands-on gardener at her family garden, Stockton Bury in Herefordshire, which regularly features in round-ups of the best UK open gardens to visit. She is also a public speaker, podcast presenter and RHS judge.

Tamsin is also a features writer for newspapers and magazines, former editor of *The English Garden* and deputy editor of *Amateur Gardening*. She is a prolific lecturer at home and abroad and her aim is to make her audiences laugh.

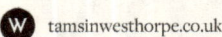 tamsinwesthorpe.co.uk   @tamsinwesthorpe   @tamsinwesthorpe

This paperback edition published in Great Britain in 2022 by Orphans Publishing

www.orphanspublishing.co.uk

Text copyright © 2020 by Tamsin Westhorpe

Illustration copyright © Hannah Madden, 2020 (flowers);
© Rosalie Herrera, 2022 (tool kit and cover illustration)

The right of Tamsin Westhorpe to be identified as the Author of the Work has been asserted by her in accordance with the Copyright, Design and Patents Act 1988.

All rights reserved. No part of this publication may be reproduced, stored in a retrieval system or transmitted, in any form or by any means, electronic, mechanical, photocopying, recording or otherwise, without the prior written permission of the publisher.

A Cataloguing in Publication record for this book is available from the British Library

Paperback: 978-1-903360-49-1

Printed and bound by Clays Ltd., Elcograf, S.p. A.

*In memory of my late father,
Robert Marston,
who famously said,
"She'll never make a living weeding."*

Contents

About the author ii
A word about this book vii
About Stockton Bury Gardens viii

FEBRUARY:
Shivering amongst the snowdrops 1
Coppicing hazel 18

MARCH:
The muddiest mother at the school gate 21
Repotting trees and shrubs 40

APRIL:
Those who see beauty are the lucky ones 43
Keeping hens and poultry 58

MAY:
I have returned unscathed from the city 61
Growing flowers for cutting 78

**SEASONAL TREATS
FOR LATE WINTER AND SPRING** 80

JUNE:
Anyone for tennis? 83
Dazzling container displays 102

JULY:
I'm just grateful they didn't head
up my trouser leg! 105
Summer garden parties 120

AUGUST:
Giggling from within the borders 123
Storing homegrown onions 138

SEPTEMBER:
The familiar smells of autumn return.. 141
Saving and storing seed 156

SEASONAL TREATS
FOR SUMMER AND EARLY AUTUMN... 158

OCTOBER:
No coming back from death by choking 161
Planting trees 178

NOVEMBER:
This garden is my free gym 181
Mastering the art of pruning.. 194

DECEMBER:
A pocket full of mucky tissues 197
A homemade country Christmas.. 210

JANUARY:
I don't hold my drink well at all.. 213
Welcoming garden birds 226

SEASONAL TREATS
FOR AUTUMN AND WINTER.. 228

Acknowledgements 230

A word about this book

I have written this book in real-time from the potting bench at Stockton Bury Gardens in Herefordshire. The garden is at the heart of a working farm, which has been in my family for over 100 years.

My great-great-grandfather bought Stockton Bury in 1886, and I am one of the fifth generation of family to work the land here; each building and patch of ground has its own story to tell. My sisters and I recall my grandmother washing the front doorstep with Lifebuoy soap and my grandfather leaning on his shepherd's crook in the farmyard smoking his pipe. My mother and my uncle have memories that go even further back, to cart horses in the stables and taking afternoon tea with their great-aunts on the main lawn.

Coming from a family with a few successful gardeners in it, I was fortunate that my parents never once tried to encourage me to become anything else – apart from a moment of madness when they signed me up for a short secretarial course. My great-uncle was John Treasure of Burford House Gardens in Tenbury Wells and he had proved that it was possible to make a career of gardening, achieving RHS Chelsea Gold medals and being awarded the RHS Victoria Medal of Honour. However, in the early 1990s gardening wasn't something that many women chose as a career. Nevertheless it was a subject that I felt connected to and, after completing some very happy years at Sparsholt College in Winchester studying horticulture, I became a parks gardener in Dorset. I was blissfully content as I mastered the art of maintaining bowling greens, creating colourful bedding schemes and even enjoyed the endless litter-picking. Weeding on windy clifftops filled my days, but my knowledge of plants was not the only thing that increased.

More importantly I learnt that gardeners were undervalued by the public. Perhaps this is not such a widespread issue today, but I believe we still have a long way to go to encourage youngsters that a wonderful, healthy and rewarding occupation can be enjoyed as a gardener. I have had a very rich and happy career in this industry and have so many colleagues to thank for their support. Gardeners should share their knowledge and enthusiasm, and this is one of the reasons I'm writing this book.

I have been lucky enough to benefit myself from this generously shared gardening wisdom. I grew up watching my uncle, Raymond Treasure, and his partner, Gordon Fenn, create Stockton Bury Gardens in the early 1980s. Each time my sisters and I returned to see our grandparents, who lived in the main house, there was a little more horticultural magic. These two remarkable gardeners, dreamers, builders and plantsmen deserve my sincere thanks for allowing me to join them in their garden. I could never claim this garden as my own – it will forever be their creation. All I can hope to do is help to look after it and continue to learn from them.

I have written this book as an enthusiastic gardener for fellow enthusiasts and my aim is to jog memories, share stories and make you smile. You'll find my personal diary of gardening along with my favourite seasonal plants and timely reminders of things you might want to tackle each month. I also hope that this book will serve up a little insight into rural life to those who have not had the pleasure of working in a country garden. It can be quite a culture shock if you're used to parks and city backyards!

About Stockton Bury Gardens

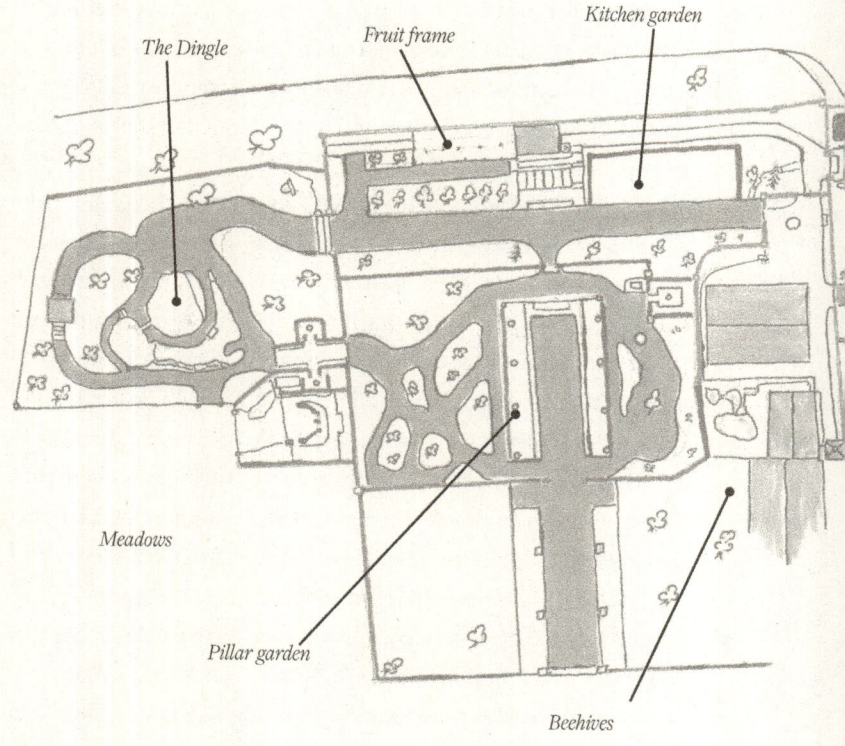

The gardens at Stockton Bury occupy a four-acre plot 320 feet above sea level. The soil is rich Herefordshire clay (perfect for potato growing) and the site is sheltered, boasting a vast collection of rare and unusual plants. It has a kitchen garden, a water garden (known as the Dingle), and a dovecote that dates back to the time of Henry I. It is laid with informal borders and garden rooms that give it an intimate feel.

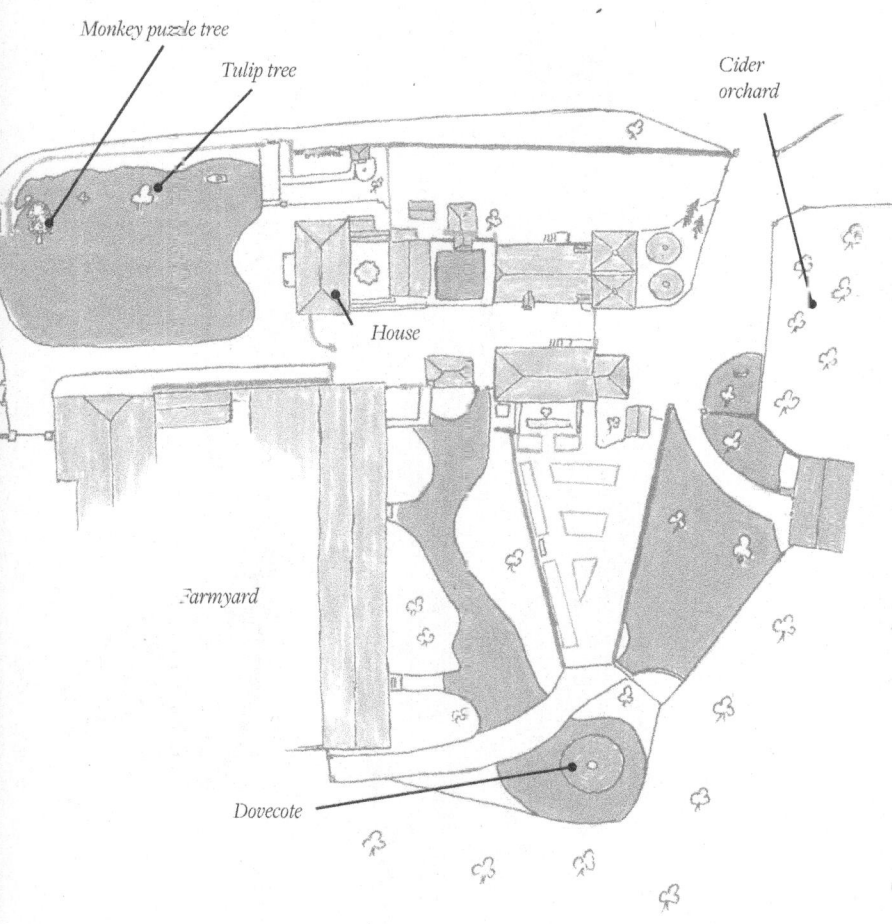

Set in the heart of a working farm, the garden is surrounded by fields and orchards. The garden and farm are strongly linked and co-exist happily side by side. Our family garden is now open during the summer, and though the plants and landscape attract visitors to the garden, it's the sense of personal history that keeps bringing them back.

Must-have plants

Cornus mas
Crocus tommasinianus
Cyclamen coum
Eranthis hyemalis
Hamamelis x intermedia
Hellebores
Iris reticulata
Mahonia
Narcissus 'Bowles's Early Sulphur'
Snowdrops
Viburnum x bodnantense 'Dawn'

FEBRUARY

Shivering amongst
the snowdrops

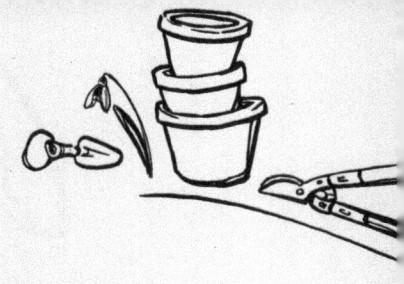

Tool Kit

Spring-tine rake: invest in a good
one that's light and easy to use.

Narrow sharp transplanting spade:
I advise a brightly coloured handle.

Good quality, waterproof kneeler
(or a grain sack stuffed with straw).

Slug and snail repellents, including organic
pellets, or two hungry call ducks.

Chicken wire: essential for rabbit-proofing
the garden.

Thin layers of clothing, and tops that
are long enough to cover your builder's
bottom. Fleece head band, thick socks,
thermal underwear and tights (attractive).

A tin of biscuits in the tool shed for those
low-sugar moments, and tea – plenty of it!

February

It's a short month with short days but it's a time for long trousers and lengthy hours in the garden. My advice is to carry on through gritted teeth and tolerate the red and running nose, frozen fingers and chilly toes. Those who think that the February garden isn't one of interest are simply not looking hard enough.

February-flowering shrubs generously share their perfume, the colourful stems of cornus and willow should be applauded and snowdrops push up through the ground however hard it is with frost. The countryside is quietly building up the energy to explode into life in spring, so this is the month to take control and concentrate on planting, pruning and propagating.

The weather is often dreadfully cold but a warm February isn't to be wished for. An early spring only races on to an early summer which can lead to a premature winter and no one wants that.

On the farm it's the start of the calving season for many farmers. At our Herefordshire farm we welcome the first of the lambs. The cattle are still tucked up in the barns and being fed morning and night – now wouldn't that be nice?

Monday 5th February

Why would you start writing a diary on February 5th? There's no good reason other than that it is too cold to garden today. As a gardener your life choices revolve around the weather – amen!

If you're reading this and haven't been gardening since Christmas (or, horrors, before!), you need to set to work. By February I've cut back all the faded perennials and my borders are pretty much clear. I've also managed to shake off any excess weight I put on over Christmas thanks to the endless trips back and forward to the compost heap with prunings, leaves and weeds. I can see the nipples of tulips poking out of my pots and there are tiny new leaves forming on the honeysuckle.

Winter-flowering plants are so valued as they're a sign of hope that spring is on the way. Beds that were bare suddenly have sparkle, thanks to the nodding heads of snowdrops and bright yolk yellow of eranthis. When you see these familiar faces you are reminded why you garden. I pity those who have left the big garden tidy-up until now, as they are likely to either tread on the newly forming shoots emerging from the ground or miss their snowdrops altogether as they're covered in the faded foliage of summer perennials.

Of course, there's a long-standing debate amongst gardeners as to whether you should cut back borders now or in the autumn. I'm autumn all the way: it's often warmer, and I like to enjoy the winter festivities without the prospect of cutting back four acres of garden hanging over me like an oversized Christmas tree bauble. Leave the borders in a large country garden until now and it's daunting.

FEBRUARY

Yes, I hear all of you who are shouting at the page about providing a home for overwintering insects, but I can assure you that there are plenty of places for our insect friends in my grassy banks, drystone walls and shrubberies. In a city garden, leaving faded foliage standing for longer is understandable, but in the country I'm all for taking action early.

In the past I have left perennials standing over winter, and you are often rewarded with attractive seed heads dusted with a sugary coating of white if the weather is dry but frosty. There's no denying that this wintery scene is dreamy, but one heavy rainstorm and the whole lot comes crashing down. Then the resulting look is far from gorgeous. So, get it all cleared early is my advice, or at least remove the plants that have gone to mush.

This winter I've been a solitary soul in the garden. My uncles pop out occasionally to join me but on the whole I'm on my own. The garden closes to the public in early October and, as a result, the atmosphere changes quite dramatically. In spring and summer I can hear the clinking of cutlery as visitors enjoy their lunch in the café, the giggles as friends chat as they stroll and the constant exchange of plant-based conversation. Now it's silent. I don't mind the silence; I've grown to quite like my own company. Gardening alone gives you plenty of time to think and look at plants and wildlife more carefully. In the drama of summer it's easy to miss out on the small but important details of a garden. Having said that, if I were to garden alone all year in silence, I'm sure I'd start to dissect my life. Company in the border occasionally is good for you

February is my preferred month for planting new shrubs if the weather is mild. Today I spent a good half an hour searching for a transplanting spade that I only used a few days ago. Had it been stolen? Unlikely! Where had it gone?

FEBRUARY

After a lot of head-scratching I found it in the tump where I put my leaves and prunings before they're transferred to the compost heap. It was well disguised, thanks to its muddy shaft. In a large garden, brightly coloured tools are certainly the more sensible option if you're prone to leaving things to come back to later! Transplanting spades are a great investment. They have a smaller, narrower head that allows you to put in or take out shrubs from tight spaces, so I'm glad I've found it. The planting of a new cornus could go ahead.

Tuesday 6th February

I've spent this evening looking at a picture of Her Majesty The Queen. Most village halls seem to have one. My challenge tonight was to persuade a room of ageing gardeners that they need to prepare for spring now.

On arrival, one garden club member announced to her friends that she was still waiting for a hip replacement. Watching me bouncing up and down with enthusiasm about pruning and planting probably wasn't what she came to see. Only one member of the audience dropped off to sleep, which is pretty good going considering the lights were turned down low.

The number of people who attended my talk was surprising as today we've had snow. Wet snow, but definitely snow. I was half expecting a call to cancel but they were a hardy bunch. After an hour of drooling over images of spring-flowering plants, I think we all felt sufficiently warmed up and reminded that winter will end and spring will be here before you know it – hopefully along with a crop of new hips!

Wednesday 7th February

This morning I've been cutting back a mature Euphorbia mellifera that had been damaged by the last heavy snowstorm.

This plant is lethal to prune as euphorbias have milky sap that can irritate the skin and can cause serious problems if any sap gets rubbed into the eyes. Goggles and gloves are a must. I've cut it to the ground in the hope it will reshoot – we'll find out together later in the year.

The rest of the day I spent raking my way through borders. I'm amazed at the signs of life at my feet. I use a Sneeboer springtine rake – the crème de la crème when it comes to rakes. Whilst working, I noticed that you can happily rake over eranthis to clear autumn leaves without causing too much damage to the flowers, but *Cyclamen coum* will be completely beheaded with one sweep of a rake. Oops! Those who have spent hours wielding a rake will understand the need to have one that's a delight to use. Before you part with any money, spend time in the garden centre weighing up your options: do you prefer a wider head, a shorter handle or a lighter weight? Choosing garden tools is a little like choosing a man – what you fancy might not be the same as your neighbour!

You might be questioning why I'm still clearing leaves, but in the country they just keep on coming. A gust of wind and your garden will soon be home to a fresh batch of oak leaves. Don't be a fool and try to collect leaves on a windy day – you'll look like a mother following a toddler! Wait for calmer weather: today was perfect, fresh and still. Over the years I've tried all sorts of techniques for clearing leaves. Petrol leaf-blowers work well but they can be hot, noisy and heavy to use. Leaf-collectors with brushes and a hopper work to some extent, but in my opinion nothing seems to beat a spring-tine rake when clearing from borders or lawns. Spending the day raking is exhausting but I console myself that it is also the perfect way to strengthen your stomach muscles. Another positive way of viewing this fresh onslaught is the chance to make leaf mould, although so far my uncle refuses to let me make a spot for this in the garden.

A morning of leaf-clearing is enough for anyone, so in the afternoon I went on the hunt for a less intensive task: pruning. To prune an unruly honeysuckle in the border I propped a ladder against the wall it was climbing up. At the top of the ladder I had the sudden urge to check my mobile phone. At last I had reached new heights and found a spot in the garden with reception! For a moment I was tempted to make a call, but then sense prevailed. On my own, six feet up a ladder with a sharp tool and on the telephone ... not a good idea. I live to see another day.

Thursday 8th February

The first lambs have arrived on our farm. All the ewes have been moved to the field and barn closest to the house. What a palaver!

Moving sheep is a skill – you need to be able to run at speed in wellies and you also need to be a mind-reader. Most farmers (my uncle included) have a clear idea of where the sheep are going, but they quite often fail to pass that on to their human sheep dogs.

After the excitement of bleating lambs, and apologising to frustrated drivers held up by our flock, I was happy to be back in the garden. The weeds are really starting to show their prowess in the borders. Rosebay willowherb is the biggest invader. I've been working in the beds under the kitchen garden wall – being brick and south-facing, it's as close to being by a radiator as possible. My advice to all fellow gardeners is to pick a job in a sunny spot in the garden, especially when icicles are hanging, as they are today. This wall is where cherries, kiwis and apricots thrive in summer, proving that even in Herefordshire a gardener can produce an interesting fruit bowl. I love this wall. It's well over 100 years old and there are so many old nails in the mortar where gardeners before me have supported plants that it looks a little like a medieval dartboard. It is also a reminder that plants come and go. We are all so shocked when we lose a mature plant, but they are living things. Yours might just have had enough of this world. Gardens are ever-evolving and that's a good thing.

Weeding is a task I find strangely satisfying but only if I'm not under any time pressure. Panic weeding never goes well! Take a good kneeler into the garden, wrap up warm, put on a pair of thin gloves and relax into your work. The comfort of your knees is crucial to this. I've tried knee-pads in the past instead of a kneeler. However, to prevent the pads from slipping down your legs when you walk, they need to be so tight that your blood circulation is often hindered, particularly when crouching. Kneelers, however, come in all shapes and sizes so there will certainly be one to make the task a pleasure. I'm in love with a large kneeler that's about 5cm thick and waterproof. It's large enough to sit comfortably on as well as kneel. If you find one that you favour, don't make the mistake of storing it in the shed. Mice seem to be trained to destroy kneelers – the filling makes wonderful nesting material. For those wanting to live the good life and avoid a garden centre till point I can highly recommend stuffing an old grain sack with

FEBRUARY

straw and tying the top with bailer twine. This makes the perfect free kneeler. The added bonus is that this is unlikely to be stolen by other members of the family.

I confess to not wearing gardening gloves as much as I should for weeding. I start with good intentions and positively rave about my new gloves on day one. After a day of weeding they are thrown into a large cooking pot that hangs on a hook in the shed. In this pan I have a collection of odd gloves. Where the other gloves go to, I have no idea. Once a year I try to match up the oddments to make pairs, but rarely do I manage to reunite a couple. My issue with some gloves (apart from their skill in disappearing) is that the following day they are crusty and stiff, and so my excitement for them fades and I resort to gloveless gardening. This is not to be recommended, especially if you want to head out into normal society at some point with hands that look halfway respectable. Gloves are the way forward, so do as I say and not as I do. Washable ones that bounce back as new after a short spin in the machine are a good option.

If I were a professional photographer I would choose to do a study of gardener's hands. Take a close look at your friends' and neighbours' hands and you'll soon see who the real gardeners are. I adore the gnarled, wrinkled and soil-engrained hands of a true gardener. These are the people who know their stuff. Perhaps this is secretly why I don't always turn to gloves, as I hanker after hands that tell the story of gardening prowess.

Wednesday 14th February

No one should be gardening on a day like this. The ground is frozen and there's icy rain. However, I am still persevering as the garden opens to the public in April and the race is on to get ready.

I wonder if any of our visitors have the first idea of how many hours we spend preparing to open the gates in spring? Last week one of my friends mentioned that she might like to try a job working outside – I'm convinced that she'd retract that comment if she was here with me today.

My aim today is to tidy up the long borders. These borders are backed with yew hedging, which is offering me a little shelter as I work. Many gardeners dream of creating matching borders, but the reality is that it doesn't work. Opposite beds have very different aspects – in short, one border will always enjoy more sun than the other. Plants will grow at different rates. When originally planted there were two shrubby potentillas at the front of each bed. The two planted on the sunny side are thriving, whilst one on the other side is dead and the other is hanging on for dear life. The only way to have successful opposite beds is to plant them differently and forget the idea of a mirror image.

Today is Valentine's Day, but you don't need me to remind you of that. This is the day I start my slug attack. A Valentine's Day massacre. If you use a few organic slug pellets now around emerging vulnerable plants, you will kill off the first generation of slugs. When you know that a slug or snail will breed about four times in a year and lay as many as 350 eggs in one year, it's no wonder that gardeners are frantically throwing the slimy beasts over their neighbours' hedges in May. Leave this job until spring and you've missed the boat.

Look out for plants that offer some slug resistance, unless you want to be on constant high alert. Don't let this put you off hostas, though. Hostas are the best value plants I know and you shouldn't be discouraged by their slug-attracting qualities. Those with blue leaves tend to be less appealing to molluscs as their leaves are often thicker. From April until mid-October hostas earn their place in a garden like nothing else.

In my opinion, as well as a judicious application of slug pellets on the most romantic day of the year, the best way to rid your country garden of slugs and snails is to invest in a couple of small call ducks. Don't let them run rampage over your whole garden or they'll end up feasting on your little seedlings, but if you have some willing children it's a great activity to entice them to collect slugs and snails: provide them with a bucket for the slippery suckers at dusk and then throw them into the duck run.

As I garden I can hear the early lambs in the field. It's been a cold start to life for them. When I am unable to identify if the water rolling down my cheeks are tears or icy rain, I retreat inside for a cup of tea. The lambs remain outside to face the elements.

Thursday 15th February

A better day. The sun is trying to show its face and the birds are singing. I have two problems, so today has a theme: GET THEM OUT.

The first problem is that there's a rabbit at large and the second is that primulas have taken over the sunken garden. I tackled the

FEBRUARY

second problem first. The morning was spent removing hundreds of primula seedlings. Leave them be and that would be all we'd have in the border, leaving no interest after they've flowered in spring. As I lift them the vine weevil grubs reveal themselves. Vine weevil eat the roots of some plants (especially heucheras and strawberries). These horrible little characters are attracted to primulas, so by removing them the pest problem should be reduced. The robin who's been watching me work all week is thankful for these juicy little grubs.

To solve the first problem is trickier. Finding out how a rabbit has managed to enter the four-acre garden is like finding a needle in a haystack. Stockton Bury is surrounded by farmland, and with farmland comes scenes of Watership Down. I start the investigation by walking the entire perimeter of the garden, looking for holes in the fencing. This entails creeping behind shrubs and getting hooked onto vicious rose bushes – I am guilty of releasing a few expletives as I untangle myself. As I search, I notice that the foliage of the bluebells has emerged. It's now really important to stay off the woodland area where they grow, to prevent stomping on the developing flowers.

Success! I find the hole in the fence and work begins. I dig a trench up against the old fence and replace the chicken-wire. About four inches of the wire is placed underground to hinder the enthusiastic digger. This won't be the last rabbit to enter the garden this year, but every small victory must be celebrated.

Rabbit problem solved, I move on to bees. There are five beehives in the paddock garden and today the bees are still. It's too cold for them to venture out, so it's my chance to cut back the rather rampant parthenocissus that covers the wall behind the hives. Having been stung in the summer, resulting in a rather unattractive swollen eyelid, I wasn't taking any chances. My ladder work pruning was undertaken in a rather dashing beekeeper's suit. Could I see through the netting to work? No. However, I'm not brave enough to prune without my netting veil.

The beehives sit on concrete slabs and at this time of year you'll see dead bees on the slabs. Last year, when I spotted the corpses, I rang the beekeeper in a panic. He quickly reassured me that any bees that die in the hive over winter are dragged out by their 'friends' and thrown out. Not a very ceremonious way to end your life. On warmer winter days those bees that are alive and well are feasting on the mahonia nectar – it's no wonder, as this reliable shrub offers a rather delicious lily-of-the-valley scent.

Having the bees in the garden certainly has its advantages but I'm grateful I'm not the one looking after them. This is a hobby that takes dedication, know-how and bravery. The hives are placed in a small orchard that adjoins the garden. The first year they arrived they were placed romantically amongst the apple trees and directly on the grass: it looked like the perfect country scene. However, if your hives are in the grass it is very tricky to have the paddock grazed by sheep. They will soon rub up against the hives. Being the over-enthusiastic fool that I am, I had insisted that I would mow the paddock instead of letting the sheep graze it as I was so keen to have the hives in this setting. I failed! I attempted it twice with the ride-on mower dressed in a full bee suit. A ride-on mower is not the answer to all your problems! My mower is often being fixed thanks to a clash with some uneven ground. They are not Land Rovers with blades and can't bounce over humps and bumps of a well-used paddock without being injured.

Admitting defeat is always painful but as a result of my unreliable mowing regime the bees now live in a pen in the paddock with a black matting base. This allows the beekeeper to work without tripping over knee-high grass and it avoids the use of power tools by the hive – some power tools cause distress to bees and they'll quickly attack the user. This pen doesn't quite offer the look I was after, but it does allow the paddock to be grazed by sheep and saves me hours of mowing on uneven ground.

Sunday 18th February

It's snowdrop season and time for the galanthophiles to gather. As I admired our crop of stunning snowdrops I was reminded of a time when I ended up at a snowdrop lunch by default.

Getting an invite to such an event isn't easy. These occasions are only for those who have a nose for snowdrops (I have a very large nose but it still doesn't fit the criteria). We have rather a special snowdrop at Stockton Bury but never show it to anyone, in fear that it might get stolen. One wonders then if there is any point having it? Now, there's a good topic for a Miss Marple mystery – Murder at the Snowdrop Party. The lunch I attended by default, I was the driver for my uncle and managed to slip in and mingle with the likes of Carol Klein. Before lunch we wandered the garden and admired the snowcrops. I compare this experience to being at a quiz night where you don't know the answer to any of the questions. My advice would be to straggle behind the experts and keep shtum.

You simply can't pretend to be a snowdrop expert – you will get found out. By the end of the walk I felt ignorant and almost rather out of love with these plants. I'm quite happy to stick to the well-known varieties and leave it at that. This is a good thing really, when you realise that some bulbs can command a huge price tag that reaches into hundreds of pounds. It's an expensive passion to indulge. The conversation over lunch was, of course, snowdrops. Again, I felt out of my depth and if the bowl of soup in front of me was large enough I'd have jumped in and swum away.

If you're keen to learn a little bit more and treat yourself to a new snowdrop then I suggest that you head somewhere that has them labelled well. Ivy Croft Nursery in Ivington, Herefordshire (yes – the Ivington where Mr Don resides) has a wonderful array of well-labelled snowdrops on sale. Having succumbed, I was advised by the experts there to sink the potted snowdrop into the ground until the foliage had turned yellow. I am then to turn it out of the pot and replant it deeper. It's rather fun to garden under the same rain cloud and in the same clay soil as Monty Don.

Things to do

- *Wash your gardening gloves.*

- *Visit a snowdrop garden. Go with a friend instead of heading for a coffee. A chat whilst you wander through snowdrops is far more enjoyable than staring at each other across a table.*

- *Make sure your garden is home to winter-flowering plants so bees can harvest nectar.*

- *Prune your autumn raspberries, wisteria and cornus that's grown for its winter stems.*

- *If you have any damaged apples in your store put them out on the lawn for the ground-feeding blackbirds.*

- *Save your old egg boxes, as they're handy for chitting potatoes.*

- *Remove the leaves of hellebores so you can see the flowers.*

FEBRUARY

Country Project

COPPICING HAZEL

Every country garden needs a row of sweet peas. To support them nothing looks better than hazel stems, and the time to coppice your hazel is at the beginning of this month.

Coppicing is the ancient woodland craft of cutting back woody plants right to the ground. This woodland craft has been used for thousands of years, and entire woodlands were coppiced before the introduction of the motor engine. Local people would lift the wood and take it home by horse and cart. Coppicing allows light to reach the ground in dense woods, which encourages wildflowers to develop. Anemones and bluebells thrive in a coppiced woodland. However, coppicing fell out of favour after the First World War and, after being unmanaged for decades, many woodlands suffered.

Happily, coppicing and woodland craft is now back in favour and it is fairly easy to buy a bundle of hazel stems. In my garden I have three hazels and each one is cut every third year. It's not unusual to have to use a chainsaw to cut them right back, but don't be tempted to use one without experience – they can be lethal. (Interestingly, tree surgeons do tend to be rather attractive for some reason, so I'll find any excuse to have them visit the garden!) The hazel stems are then stored in a dark shed and used as plant supports for clematis and sweet peas. I'm not quite sure how I'd cope without my bundle of hazel poles in the shed.

How to train roses using hazel supports

Within the herbaceous borders we have some impressive shrub roses such as 'Gertrude Jekyll'. To encourage a bumper crop of flowers we train them with hazel stems. Once trained, they look like giant spiders in the border.

1. Cut your hazel stems to the length of 2m.
2. About 1m away from the crown of the rose, push the end of a hazel stem into the ground.
3. Bend the stem over and push the other end into the ground near the heart of the plant. (This is tricky as the stem can easily act as a catapult! You have been warned.)
4. Tie one rose stem to the arched hazel with twine.
5. Repeat with at least four hazel stems, creating hazel arches that surround the rose, and tie a rose stem to each support.
6. Wait patiently! I promise that, in due course, along the top of each cane you'll have roses like never before.

Must-have plants

Anemone nemorosa

Chaenomeles speciosa 'Moerloosei'

Corydalis solida

Epimedium versicolor

Fritillaria meleagris

Hepatica nobilis

Lathyrus vernus

Magnolia stellata

Muscari armeniacum (I love the pale blue 'Valerie Finnis')

Narcissus (dwarf types such as 'Minnow' and 'Jetfire' are gorgeous)

Ribes sanguineum

Tropaeolum tricolor

MARCH

The muddiest mother at the school gate

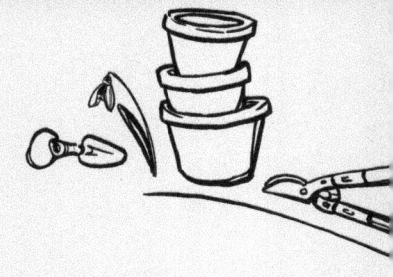

Tool Kit

*Seed-sowing equipment and seed compost
(don't expect your seed to cope with a
multi-purpose compost).*

Ericaceous feed for your potted blueberry plants.

*An old metal barrel that can be transformed
into a rhubarb forcer.*

*A working mower: get yours serviced, and if you're
ordering a new one do it at the beginning of this
month and not the end. You'll need it soon.*

*Thin gloves for fine weeding, small hand rake and
new batteries for the radio – with the weeds coming
thick and fast you might as well settle into the job.*

*A good waterproof with ventilation
(or you'll be a stinky mess by the
end of a busy day in the garden!).*

March

Anything can happen this month. Weather extremes are to be expected. I'm constantly splattered in mud and there really doesn't seem much point washing your gardening clothes every night. Dry them on the Aga and the mud will soon brush off!

After a fairly solitary winter I'm suddenly joined by the smiling faces of native primulas and the bleating of lambs coming thick and fast. Farmers are spending sleepless nights in the lambing sheds and the team at *The Archers* are bound to be hunkering down too with sleeping bags and flasks of tea. The iconic Radio 4 show is actually a great way for a country novice to stay on top of the farming issues of the day, so take your radio outdoors and settle into some gardening with the goings on in Ambridge to entertain you.

Signs of new life are everywhere and I wouldn't want to be anywhere else. I don't even mind the slight whiff of slurry that drifts on the country air – it's all part of this rural idyll.

For most of the month I'll have my head down in the borders looking for emerging weeds. It's vital that I take hold of the garden now, as once plants start to burst into life they will be stronger than I am. There's no end of things to do but the most important is to watch how rapidly things change around you. Don't sleepwalk through the arrival of spring – hop, skip and jump through it instead.

Thursday 1st March

March has arrived, but it has characteristics more akin to January. We are knee-deep in snow. My snowdrops and eranthis are buried under drifts and the lambs in the fields are sheltering up against the hedges.

Snow is no good for gardening or farming. Fortunately, gardens can cope without the gardener for a few days, but farmers must continue with their duties whatever the weather.

The only thing a gardener can do in weather like this is clear heavy snow off hedges, polytunnels and greenhouses. Thankfully this snow is light and fluffy, and the wind has swept most of it from trees and shrubs already. The last lot we had in January caused great damage in the garden and I had to cut back our *Romneya coulteri* (Californian tree poppy) right to the ground, as the weight of the snow snapped many of its branches. This impressive plant is perfect for a sheltered spot with a well-drained soil – but even when planted in those perfect conditions it can't always cope with a huge dump of snow. In summer it offers large white petals that look like a tissue paper skirt to the yolk-yellow centre – bring on the summer!

At this time of year, most gardening magazines and blogs will suggest that you sit by your Aga on a cold day and flick through seed catalogues. Follow this advice with caution – you'll fall in love with so many plants that you'll never have time to sow them all. After all, how much seed does one gardener need? I also warn those who, like me, might be suffering from chilblains not to actually put their feet up against the Aga. Thanks to the continued cold weather and the fact that I live in a draughty house with flagstone floors, I have developed chilblains on my feet. Most gardeners will suffer from them at some point. An elderly gentleman shared his advice on this ailment with me this week and it has almost cured the ill. He recommended wearing tights – simple. If you garden without thermal long johns or tights and your legs get cold, he told me, you'll be in trouble. I had just been wearing several pairs of socks. The extra layer on my legs has helped me put to use a rather ugly pair of woollen tartan tights I've had in my drawer for many years (possibly decades).

I'm a huge fan of appropriate underwear when gardening. Long-sleeved vests are a must, and large Bridget Jones-style knickers are not to be dismissed. In fact, anything that keeps my lower back warm is good with me. When the temperature dips, lots of thin layers and a sheepskin bodywarmer are my chosen attire. In summer, however, I'm all for gardening with as little on as possible, and I have been known to work in my bra (and why wouldn't you? My mother was often known to garden similarly unclothed so this is a fashion statement I inherited from her.).

Monday 5th March

The snow is thawing quickly but whilst the garden is tucked up under its white duvet, I'm tidying the shed. This shed is special and intriguing enough to feature in a Harry Potter film – it's magical.

Nothing much has changed about this shed since I was a child. It's home to plenty of completely useless secateurs that for some reason we never throw out and a rather wonderful collection of small terracotta pots, antique and very rusty mole traps, odd gloves and a small cooker. The small terracotta pots are what young tomato plants were supplied in when my uncle was a boy. What a joy to receive a young plant in a warm and welcoming clay pot. You never know, this way of supplying plants might return as we look for a plastic-free alternative. Resting on the bench is an old table-top cooker. I've always wondered what the cooker was there for but, inexplicably, had never opened the oven door until today. On opening it, I discover where my uncle stores his seed. Genius – there's no chance that a mouse will get in there. This made me think that an old microwave could be the perfect store for seed stacked in airtight boxes. With such a large seed store I suppose you wouldn't need to exercise restraint – so put your feet up against the Aga and order to your heart's content!

The reason for the tidy-up of the shed is that I have a gardening apprentice starting tomorrow. This organised state won't last, I'm sure, but at least I can give the right first impression. I wonder if she will be as nervous as I am – will she expect me to know the Latin name of every plant in the garden? If she does, she'll be sorely disappointed. The older I get the more I realise how little I know. This evening I shall pack my car with projector, computer and extension lead and head off to talk at a garden club. I hope I do not disappoint there either, although I am taking solace in the fact that I'm pretty sure few will come to listen to me due to the weather.

Tuesday 6th March

I have returned triumphant! The further I trekked from home last night the worse the snow drifts got and I felt like an intrepid explorer. I was prepared for anything – I'd had a bowl of porridge before leaving and there was a blanket and spade in the boot.

What I wasn't prepared for, though, was a crowd. On arrival panic set in. The car park was full, and the hall was packed with over 100 people. My emergency spade was no help to me now! It was time to put my best foot forward and put on a show. I've learnt over the years that you can't know everything and at last, after years of giving gardening talks, I'm no longer intimidated by the knowledgeable. Admitting that you don't know the answer to a question is far better than trying to fudge it. After all, when it comes to gardening there is usually more than one correct answer to a question anyway.

The talks I give at garden clubs give me a great deal of pleasure. Each and every hall offers an unusual quirk and I always have some entertaining story to share with my completely uninterested husband who, by the time I return home from far-flung corners of the countryside, is usually tucked up in bed. He is at a total loss as to why I drive so far to talk to fellow gardeners and return in the dead of night, but I enjoy each and every occasion. I've had a chairman pass out when introducing me; I've been party to the odd internal argument at AGMs about whose turn it is to make the teas and I've had a power cut in the middle of the talk and had to continue by candlelight – on occasion it is like being at a live show run by the late Victoria Wood and Julie Walters.

If you want a true taste of the countryside, I highly recommend you join your local garden club. Some are struggling for members and I for one would be very sad to see a further decline. Go and meet the locals, learn about plants and quietly take in the glorious display of personalities at work. I can't think of a better way of enjoying an evening out.

Friday 9th March

I'm not going to dress this up in any way – today my main focus was the toilets at Stockton Bury. When you open a garden to the public, toilets are everything. After a day with mop and bucket my facilities are exemplary. Why some people are so upset about cleaning toilets I will never know.

Satisfied with my morning's work, I later retreated to the herb bed. The scent of rosemary on a cold day is far more inviting than that of bleach! The herb garden was replanted last year. Woody herbs such as rosemary, sage and lavender have a sell-by date and once they start to get very woody and bare-stemmed, you'd be wise to replant. When planting a herb bed there are a few rules to follow.

- Pick a sunny spot with a well-drained soil.
- Grow only what you will actually use in the kitchen.
- Make sure you can easily harvest the herbs; if it's a large bed, add some stepping stones, so you can access the back of the border.

Having dug over the bed this time last year I disturbed many seeds that had been lying dormant in the soil. This disturbance encouraged them to germinate. I now have a mass of foxgloves and verbascums. The foxgloves will remain but I'm being brutal with the verbascums. They've made a home far too close to the edge of the bed and I can't stand seeing them shredded by the mullein moth in summer that they most certainly won't avoid. It's all very well planning to keep a close eye on the caterpillars of the mullein moth but they move in almost overnight and I'm often too late to pick them off.

Elsewhere in the garden the early chaenomeles flowers were irreparably damaged by the snow, the hepaticas are in flower in the alpine house and the pots of *Tropaeolum tricolor* are the highlight of the polytunnel. The chaenomeles will survive but my disappointment of missing out on a year's flowers will be long-lived. Sweet peas are starting to germinate and whilst our snowdrops are coming to an end, pots of tulips are growing at a pace. Even though the beds have been covered in snow for a good week the blessed weeds still succeed in germinating – there is so much to be done. My new fellow gardener Colette is a delight. I'm enjoying the novelty of having someone to talk to as I work. Maybe gardening shouldn't be a solitary pastime? If we hadn't been gardening all autumn and winter, there would certainly be panic here as our open season fast approaches. The garden has to be ready for our early April opening.

Monday 12th March

This week saw panic sweep across the garden. A rabbit was spotted on the main lawn. This is a complete disaster!

It's tempting to let my Border terrier Larry (otherwise known as the Wire Brush) loose, but I fear he may cause just as much damage in the garden as the rabbit! I have never known a rabbit to be as brazen as this – very brave to venture this close to the house. Someone must have left a gate open, but no one is owning up.

This week has been one of questions. Being a panellist for a charity Q&A got the cogs in my brain turning and Colette, who joins me two days a week, has plenty of questions too. I'm not sure if I'm teaching her much but one thing is certain, it's great to not be the only chicken scratching amongst the plants. At this time of year, I feel like a hen looking for worms as I work through the borders on hands and knees with a small hand rake. As we scratch, our main topic of conversation is the weeds. I know that sounds dull but we're happy.

Thursday 15th March

Today the sun shone and for the first time this year I have been gardening without a jumper. Is spring on the way?

It is certainly much later in arriving than last year, and I am gardening with caution as the weather could easily take a turn for the worse. Being a gardener is quite like being the captain of a ship. One day you're sailing across calm waters and the next you're battening down the hatches and hanging on for dear life. The old crinkled leaves that cover the gunnera crown and offer protection from the frost are still firmly in place and my tender plants remain under wraps in the polytunnel just in case.

The soil is too wet to work, really, but as the garden opens in a few weeks I'm forging ahead anyway. This makes for sticky work and on leaving the garden today I looked like I'd been wrestling in the mud with a prop forward. The only benefit of a wet soil I have found is that dandelions tend to pull out easier – the whole root just slips out of the soil. Small mercies.

The low-growing woodland plants are starting to put on a show with chionodoxa, violets, hepaticas and primulas adding spots of colour. The tiny flowers of the violets and buttery yellow colours of the primulas are favourites of mine. With so many new varieties of plants available it's easy to get swept up by the razzmatazz but simple flowers shouldn't be passed over. *Fritillaria meleagris* are only a few days off blooming – these will be very attractive to the bees. The petals of the bell-shaped flowers with their checkerboard markings look at their best for such a short time that you really need to have a camera at the ready and get down on hands and knees to get the best shot. Offering such refined beauty, I think this plant deserves us all to drop to our knees.

The monkey puzzle tree – a plant on a much larger scale – is showering the garden with its needles. I'm not impressed! It was an exceptional year for cones last year, but they are now falling apart and covering the lawn again, leaving me with the job of clearing them up. I am always slightly entertained when I see a monkey puzzle planted right outside a house because these trees grow big: according to Google they can live for up to 1,000 years. The monkey puzzle on the main lawn here was planted by my great-great-grandfather in 1886 when he purchased the property. These trees were a status symbol of the time and, looking at the date of the planting, our tree could well be the result of seed that plant-hunter William Lobb shot off the tree he found in Chile so he could bring its splendour home. I have no evidence to confirm this, but it's rather lovely to believe it might be true.

If you get up close to the giant trunk of a monkey puzzle, you'll spot the sap. When I think back to my childhood, I have so many memories of this garden, but a particularly vivid one revolves around this tree. As children, my sisters and I would pick off the sap that dribbles from the monkey puzzle tree. We quickly discovered that it was like superglue and were suitably told off for sticking our fingers together and – even worse – gettting it in our hair. I also remember making a habit of collecting the snails that hid under the aubrietia. These were stored in a Fox's biscuit tin and placed under my bed. They were my much-loved pets: I gave them fresh foliage and made plenty of air holes in the lid of the tin. I once put a handful of these snails in my primary school teacher's desk drawer. This did not go down at all well. To this day I remember her scream.

I also recall my grandmother drying walnuts to pickle on old white sheets. Once pickled they looked like miniature brains but tasted like heaven. The drive is where we all learnt to ride our bikes (some better than others – my elder sister did a spectacular head-first manoeuvre into the rose bed). The raised lawn that sits just alongside the drive is where my uncle would run to throw himself onto his rather unruly but striking hunter. We'd watch him energetically trot up the drive – he was just as impressive as the horse back then. I know how lucky I am to have memories of a happy childhood here and this is what drives me to keep this place alive. It is truly a tragedy when a family home and garden is sold, or a garden gets lost in time.

The snowdrop season is nearly at an end. The last to put on a show here is the large snowdrop 'Augustus'. However tempting it might be to cut back the foliage now that the flowers have faded – refrain. Cutting back the foliage of any bulb before it turns yellow means its performance will be weak the following year. Don't be one of those who ties the faded foliage of daffodils in knots – just let the foliage fall about freely. If I see this in a garden I have to do everything in my power to stop myself from leaping over the fence and untidying them or even worse unplaiting them! If you really can't stand unruly, yellowing foliage then grow bulbs in pots and hide the pot behind the shed when the flowers have faded.

Saturday 17th March

The scratching in the flower borders with small hand rakes continues in very wet soil. We don't turn the soil in the borders here, as they are packed with plants.

This has its advantages: if you create a bed of loose soil you are creating a perfect bed in which weeds will germinate. At Stockton Bury we are surrounded by fields, and there's always plenty of thistle seeds floating about on the country breeze in summer looking for a comfy place to call home.

The rain and cold temperatures have not subsided and gardening this month has been a messy business. Looking at the images of the garden that I took this time last year I am estimating that we are three weeks behind. The trickiest part of gardening in this weather is ridding your boots of the mud you collect. This is very important when on the school run. I must be the muddiest mother at the school gate, which is highly embarrassing for my son. To help me be just slightly respectable my car is a moving wardrobe. In the boot are spare jeans, jumpers and shoes, and in desperate times I have been known to de-robe with only the open car door as a screen. This is what happens when you don't garden where you live (my home is a couple of miles from Stockton Bury). The upside to this is that when you do go out looking respectable for once, people are often complimentary about your non-gardening attire – the contrast is just too much for them to ignore.

To make a change from scratching, I've been fighting a monster. This monster is the semi-evergreen invasive climber *Akebia quinata*. Over the last ten years it has romped its way all over a fence and it is time to take control. It will root wherever a stem touches the soil; after two days of clearing the result is a tractor trailer full of the climber. It had encroached into the bed where the rhubarb is planted. If you're thinking of planting rhubarb, then you'll need more than one crown (an established plant that's a year old). Ideally, you should plant three and force one of them every year in rotation. Forcing a plant only once in three years will allow it to rest. Cover your rhubarb every year with a forcer and the plant will quickly become exhausted and susceptible to pests and diseases. If you're looking for an early crop, then plant 'Timperley Early' or how about 'Champagne' – I love the idea of growing a plant with this bubbly name. Whichever you choose, plant in spring or autumn and in late April make sure you have adequate custard at the ready. I personally hate custard (reminds me of school) so I prefer my rhubarb cooked with brown sugar and a splash of Amaretto.

There are beautiful rhubarb forcers here in the garden but I'm going to let you into a secret: there's no rhubarb under them. Our terracotta forcers are just for decoration. Our rhubarb is forced using an old metal dustbin that the bottom has rusted out of, and the top is covered with old roof slates. As our crop is planted out of sight of our visitors it doesn't need to be pretty, and it seems a shame to hide our lovely terracotta forcers from view. How vain of us.

Monday 19th March

Frogspawn is now very evident in the ponds. It bobs around in the water like an alien life form and is in danger from hungry passing birds. At the start of March the small pond looked like a boiling cauldron. There was so much frog activity the water was almost bubbling.

It's the adult frogs that are in danger from me. As I cut back faded perennials I'm keen to avoid decapitating one. They are good at disguising themselves, so gardeners need to be on red alert. You won't live with the guilt if you injure one of the slug-eating army.

Today has been a day of showers then sunshine and I'm reminded of my grandmother's old kitchen clock. On the hour a lady would pop out of a door and then reverse back in – that lady was me today. My jeans are thick with mud and it is days like this that convince me that a pair of proper garden trousers is money well spent. Wet jeans are never comfortable; as the hours pass they get longer and longer and start dragging on the ground.

Hand-weeding gravel paths has been my task today. Some would say boring, but I find it very satisfying. The only downside to this job is that it often leads to a torn thumb nail. A small tear halfway down your nail is something you just have to get used to as a gardener. I have also taken the plunge today and put my agaves in pots back out in the garden. A trifle early but they've been placed in a south-facing spot. They've spent the winter in the polytunnel but before putting them to bed for the winter, I failed to remove the many leaves from various deciduous trees (mainly oak) that had lodged in the crown of the plant. Trying to get leaves out from the jaws of this sharp plant by hand is not to be recommended. It was Colette who suggested with a giggle that we should get the vacuum cleaner out. Laugh not, as this did just the trick! Henry Hoover is now a part of the gardening team here.

Thursday 22nd March

Now the weather is a bit milder the cattle that have spent the winter undercover are being released into the fields.

A warning – these powerful beasts have been tucked up for months and freedom is a thrill. I would highly recommend (footpath or not) that you don't walk through a field of cattle at this time of year, especially not with a dog. Having grown up on a farm, I wouldn't dream of it.

I'd also advise staying clear of fields with sheep at this time of year, as some will be lambing outside. The last thing an expectant mother needs is to be frightened by you and your pooch. I'm all for walking in the countryside but so many of us are out of touch with the farming year. This is the month to enjoy the country lanes instead. If you want to fit into a farming and country community then think about your actions and follow the Countryside Code. One last pro tip – always climb a farm gate from the hinge end to prevent it from dropping.

Sunday 25th March

Only a few days until the garden is open to visitors and the veg patch is letting the side down. It's a mess and, although working a heavy clay soil in the wet is not to be recommended (it damages the structure of the soil), I must tackle it.

The skeletons of Brussels sprouts stems remain in the patch; under a bed of straw lie carrots yet to be lifted. Usually the carrots are lifted in autumn and stored in the cellar under the house, where they are covered in a wet towel in an old wheelbarrow. Stored this way, the carrots will last until Christmas. This year we tried covering them in straw and leaving them in the ground. Sadly, this has only been a success for the mice – the straw attracted them and provided a warm bed and a veg feast all in one.

The carrots are lifted and only a few are vaguely edible at this point. The best are put in a bucket for my mother to master – she can turn even the most slug-nibbled veg into a delicious gardener's soup. The sprouts are pulled up along with the last of the parsnips. This leaves only some young onions and a row of broad beans that were planted direct in November. Yes, I did mean to say November. My uncle has planted a row of 'Aquadulce' on his birthday (15th November) since he was a boy. Through snow, frost and heavy rain, they always manage to make it and produce an early crop. Another row will be planted in late spring to ensure a double helping. Nothing is better than a young broad bean. If I were a millionaire and money were no object, I would have young broad beans on tap, alpaca socks and salted Lurpak butter to melt over the beans. Life's simple pleasures.

    I love to dig the vegetable patch, especially as the soil in the borders is never turned. It's hard work but for some reason I am always so thrilled to see the weed-free, well-turned soil – this is satisfaction indeed. I'm not troubled by bare soil, in fact, I like it. I put this down to my very happy experience of working in a parks department in my late teens. We would prepare the many beds for bedding plants and this to me felt like sculpting the soil. I associate neat edges, straight lines and bare soil with older, male gardeners so it's fair to say that I'm not a typical female gardener who might prefer rambling roses and banks of wildflowers. The idea of a romantic natural garden with blurred edges does appeal to me, but only if I'm not looking after it. It's hard to create and control a garden with blurred lines and, although it's difficult for me to admit it, I am a control freak. Although I don't turn the soil in the borders here the idea of a no-dig veg patch fills me with horror. I'm sure that the practice works but looking at a compacted plot is not something I relish. I want to run my rake through a well-turned soil and if I get a few weeds by choosing this more traditional option then so be it.

Thursday 29th March

The end of March is upon us and the weather has still not picked up. To make me feel as if summer will arrive at some point, I've been sowing seed.

Black-eyed Susans are the lucky seeds that got pulled from their tomb to be brought to life. By tomb, I mean my kitchen drawer. Being a garden writer and an avid consumer of gardening magazines I have stashes of cover-mounted free seed packets everywhere.

Today is the first time the lawns have been cut. The grass has been very slow to get going this year and the turf laid to fill in bare patches has taken its time to settle. If I had to choose just a few things to do before opening the garden to the public it would be to sweep the drive, edge the lawns and mow. It's quite incredible how a good lawn can save any garden. I'm horrified when I hear people say that they are thinking about lifting their lawn and replacing it with a gravel garden to 'save work'. In my opinion it will just make different, worse work. It will quickly become a cat litter tray and you'll trek gravel into the house in the soles of your shoes. Plus, you can't walk barefoot on gravel. I'm all for different types of lawns. In a country garden paths mown through a meadow of grass and wildflowers is the dream. This is not easy to achieve but it's certainly worth the effort.

Magnolia stellata is in flower and as I admire the white blooms it seems like only yesterday that I was admiring its silver, fluffy young buds in October. Also in flower is the much under-valued *Lathyrus vernus*. This is a low-growing spring pea that's as tough as old boots and flowers for about four weeks. Before you ask, it isn't scented – you can't have it all.

Things to do

- *Stay glued to the weather forecast – be on frost alert.*

- *March is a great month for planting and creating new herbaceous borders. Lift and divide perennials, swap plants with friends and keep a cardboard box in the back of the car for impulse plant purchases.*

- *Repair your lawn with either seed or turf and forget any ideas you had about getting rid of it as country gardeners must have a lawn.*

- *Leave ponds alone as the frogspawn is now forming, and look out for frogs and toads when using sharp tools in the garden.*

- *Plan your veg patch. If you haven't dug in any organic matter then step to it now, and plant out chitted potatoes.*

- *It's nesting season for birds so avoid cutting hedges.*

MARCH

Country Project

REPOTTING TREES AND SHRUBS

When was the last time you treated your loyal box plant in the pot by your front door to some fresh compost? In most cases – if the owner is honest – it will be years since it last had any love.

A few years ago, I was asked by a neighbour if I could look at her struggling phormium. She was concerned that it might be under the weather. Upon arrival, I discovered that it had lived in the same pot of compost for over a decade and it hadn't been fed even once. I quickly persuaded her that this plant was far from a failure – in fact, it was a superhero. On closer inspection, the compost resembled cigarette ash. All the goodness had gone: the plant was starving.

Although many small trees and shrubs can survive without any care, they do need attention to flourish – don't we all? I beg you, remove your loyal shrub from its pot and replace the compost. (A word on compost – some shrubs will prefer an ericaceous compost, so do your research first, and always make sure it is peat-free.) Give it some feed this month and every March from now on. Once you've completed this task you might even hear the plant breathe a sigh of relief.

MARCH

How to pot on trees and shrubs

Anything will grow in a pot if given the right care. It might never give as good a show as if it were in the ground, but with a little bit of care and attention, you'll stand a far better chance.

1. Remove the plant from its pot. This isn't always easy – if a pot has been home to a shrub or tree for many years it might take two of you to ease it out. If you have an urn-shaped pot you might even have to break it in order to free the roots (this shape isn't ideal for perennials). If you need a new pot, get one ready. If you repot regularly you will probably get away with using the same pot if it was generous to begin with. Any pot you choose must have adequate drainage holes.

2. Mix some slow-release feed into your chosen compost. Put a small amount of the new compost and feed mix in the bottom of the pot, enough so that the plant will sit at the right level.

3. Loosen and knock off as much of the old compost as possible from around the plant's root ball. You can take a saw to the root ball and cut off a chunk from the bottom. This means you don't need a larger pot each time. Then place the plant back into the pot on top of the fresh compost.

4. Fill the gaps around the root ball with new compost and firm in well. Ensure that the plant isn't sitting too high in the pot, as this would make watering tricky. Try to keep the compost line about 2cm from the top of the pot.

5. Water generously.

Must-have plants

Brunnera macrophylla
Camassia quamash
Clematis alpina
Erythronium 'Pagoda'
Fritillaria imperialis
Fritillaria meleagris
Hyacinthoides non-scripta (bluebells)
Lamium orvala
Primula vulgaris
Smyrnium perfoliatum
Trilliums
Tulips
Uvularia grandiflora

APRIL

Those that see beauty
are the lucky ones

Tool Kit

A *water butt to collect abundant April showers.*

Plant supports and tree ties – get ahead and buy now – you'll need them.

Seed, seed compost and yet more seed! Go on, try a different variety of tomato this year. (But don't sow the whole packet. You only need about five tomato plants, not 50!)

Well-rotted organic matter to dig into your vegetable beds.

Strawberry plants. They only tend to be productive for about three years, so invest in new ones.

A fly swat. In warm weather the first flies will hatch out.

Easter eggs for the annual egg hunt in the garden.

April

There is no excuse for anyone to be bored in April – there's so much to be done in the country garden. There's new life all around us with lambs bouncing about the fields, hens sitting patiently on their eggs and seedlings springing up everywhere.

The grass is lush and the soundtrack of the countryside includes the hum of lawnmowers. Now's the time that anyone with a horse or pony needs to be on red alert. Leave your four-legged friend out in the paddock for too long to feast on the green stuff and it will be at risk from laminitis – a crippling disease of inflammation throughout the body, often caused by too much rich spring grass, that can be fatal.

The farmer-gardener can be working all hours during April. Sadly there's bound to be a few tiddlers (lambs rejected by their mothers) being bottle-fed morning, noon and night. You can always spot tiddlers later in life: they're so friendly they're impossible to herd! Oilseed rape is in flower, so the pollen count is high. Yellow also seems to be the dominant colour in the garden, with primroses, daffodils and caltha adding sunshine.

For me, when the garden opens this month, it's the start of a season of answering endless horticultural questions. It's at this time of year that you realise you've forgotten the names of half the plants in the garden. By the time I get to grips with all the plants of spring the summer will arrive, and along with it the next tranche of Latin names. As for the weather, anything can happen, so get those shorts, waterproofs, woolly hats and crop tops at the ready.

Sunday 1st April

The garden opened to the public today, and a few keen and regular visitors trickled in. Being April Fool's Day, the mood is rather jolly.

April has so much to offer, with early woodland plants such as *Anemone nemorosa*, fritillarias, epimediums and corydalis in flower. It's my favourite time of the year for visiting gardens; you can see the bones of the plot and the curves of borders, and admire the big spring awakening of plants, such as ferns unfurling. You can almost watch the growth of plants by the minute. This is a month full of so much hope and excitement. It's also fast-moving, so don't miss a moment of it.

Sadly, many people choose to stay in their centrally-heated homes rather than put on an extra layer, endure the unpredictable weather and admire this magical time. I can't tell you how often I've heard, "We won't come into the garden today as there won't be anything in flower yet," as a visitor heads to the café for a large slice of cake. I have decided that some people see beauty and others don't. Some do not see the wonders of nature and manage to just pass through unaffected whilst others are moved by discovering emerging plants and dainty flowers. Those that see are the lucky ones. Not, of course, that there's anything wrong with enjoying cake!

Friday 6th April

April showers are certainly not in short supply at the moment. Wellies have never been more essential.
Some plants seem to be relishing this wet spring, which is following a winter with three bouts of snow. The martagon lilies and the spotted orchids are appearing at a rate of knots, which only goes to show that wet and cold can certainly benefit some plants. Some, though, need a rather warmer temperature to thrive.

The fuchsias that have over-wintered in the cellar are now stretching their arms in the greenhouse. These old and gnarled specimens have spent the last twenty winters in our underground cave, where it stays at a constant 6°C whatever the weather. The fuchsias are always placed by the entrance to the cellar, so they have much needed light. According to my mother, I too spent time in this cellar as a baby. My grandfather would instruct my mother to put me in the cellar in my large Silver Cross pram, so that they could enjoy their Sunday dinner in peace. He was from the seen and not heard generation – well, in his case, 'not seen and not heard'! To be fair, I'm told I was a particularly noisy baby. I recently stood in the cellar and shouted – wow, what an echo! I can only assume that my cries would have been very dramatic down here. Childcare methods may have moved on, but I came through unscathed. The base and wheels of that very pram have now been transformed into my son's garden go-kart. As a family we are exemplary at recycling and, fortunately, our childcare skills have been given a makeover too.

Joining the fuchsias in the unheated greenhouse are pleiones, arisaemas and my favourite climber, *Tropaeolum tricolor*. A plant that offers so much to this space and is rarely praised is the coleus. These tender foliage plants illuminate the greenhouse in high summer with their lime green, maroon and golden foliage but can be relied upon to add colour from this month onwards. By midsummer, this small glass box will be a treasure trove of colour and scent, and a place where I will need to work my magic with a dustpan and brush every day – fuchsias happily fling their faded flowers about with wild abandon.

Speaking of dustpans, the conversation around the Sunday dinner table recently was of this very item. The rather dented metal dustpan that I use in the garden every day was given to my late grandmother and grandfather from my great-aunt as a wedding present. It's now over 75 years old – you can only just see that it once sported an orange coat of paint. Has a wedding present ever been so long-lived? (I wonder, though, if the bride and groom were thrilled to receive it?) To say that things are archaic here is an understatement. The world may be moving at speed, but at Stockton Bury we have the brakes firmly on – so much so that sometimes I fear the tyres may be burning!

Sunday 8th April

I'm still giggling now. Last night I did a talk to a gardening club about preparing for spring. Before I began, a lady asked me how she could protect her plants from frost. I suggested that she covered them in fleece.

Upon hearing that, she pulled at her husband's sleeve and said to me, with a completely straight face, "I don't think I want to put my husband's fleece in the garden – this is his favourite jumper." How lovely, and what an insight for me – one must never assume knowledge.

APRIL

The highlight of the garden for me this week are the chaenomeles. You may recall that the flowers of some were damaged earlier in the year by the cold, but the later-flowering types escaped that chilling blast. The best of them all is *C. speciosa* 'Moerloosei'. It used to be called 'Apple Blossom', and it really does look like its namesake, so I was rather sad to discover that it is no longer officially called that – no wonder we're all confused by plant names. Whatever you like to call them, these wall shrubs are perfect companions for a south-facing wall. We should all plant more wall shrubs; they soften the sharp lines of a building and act as the plants that fuse house and garden together. My favourite is *Schizophragma hydrangeoides* 'Roseum'. In summer its flowers resemble those of a lacecap hydrangea, but they have the addition of pale pink outer florets. We have this plant growing successfully on a north wall. In April the leaves are only just starting to appear but the woody framework looks rather impressive.

The wood anemones are a triumph right now, with the white *Anemone nemorosa* 'Wilks' Giant' and the pale 'Blue Beauty' stealing the show on the grassy banks. In a week or two they will be joined by the double-white flowers of the breathtaking Anemone nemorosa 'Vestal'. By the pond, the American skunk cabbage is putting on a stink. It's now on the Invasive Plant List but here it seems to be fairly restrained. Its impressive yellow spathes appear first and then its equally attractive leaves follow. And yes, it does stink of old cabbage. Delightful Another plant that rivals it for bright yellow charm and enjoys the damp soil is Caltha palustris, but thankfully that doesn't smell of rotting veg.

Frogspawn is still aplenty in the pond. It's almost bubbling just under the surface of the water. Seeing it reminds me of my childhood. In my day, it was acceptable to collect jars of frogspawn and study it, but there is far less around here than there used to be. I clearly recall seeing it as a child in the puddles of badly drained fields on the farm. This must be a sure sign that our environment is changing, and not for the better.

Monday 16th April

The garden isn't open on a Monday so it's a good day to take stock. Most plants are growing at such a pace but some are still hiding their virtues for now.

Some of the trees still remain leafless and others, such as *Prunus padus* 'Colorata', are displaying wonderful blossom. A tree that takes its time to show any sign of life here is *Cladrastis sinensis*. Its leaves don't appear until early June!

As I sweep the greenhouse, I'm overwhelmed by the perfume of the freesias that are happily growing in terracotta pots that have been broken and glued back together many times over. I rather love the cracks – they each have a story to tell. After the perfume of roses, freesia is most definitely my favourite garden scent. I'm not much of a fan of the scent of the hyacinths that are flowering in the borders now. I prefer hyacinths presented in terracotta pots at Christmas rather than in the garden.

As a child, every cupboard I opened in autumn seemed to be home to hyacinths being forced. They look out of place to me in a garden setting – imagine Barbara Cartland in the crowd at Glastonbury Festival!

It's now that you can see if the spring bulbs you planted in autumn have come good. I'm relieved that the hundreds of *Narcissus* 'Sir Winston Churchill' I planted have shown their faces. Don't tell anyone, but as the ground was so full of tree roots I popped more than one in some of the holes. Well, no one was looking and it was cold.

'Sir Winston' is a double that offers a fantastic scent. It's quite tall at about 40cm so don't be tempted to plant it in shallow pots, like I did last year. Tall bulbs in shallow pots only end up flopping to the side very quickly.

Wednesday 18th April

Well, well, well. The sun is finally out! Temperatures rose today to about 24°C and what a shock to my plants that was. Anything in a pot looked as surprised as I was to feel the sun on my face.

This heat will certainly accelerate growth. The corylopsis is at the start of its last week of flowers and the daffodils are starting to flag. They'll soon be overtaken by the charm of *Lamium orvala*, erythroniums, uvularia, trilliums, *Lathyrus vernus* and *Dicentra cucullaria* (gosh, these all sound rather gynaecological). The lamium I mention is a dead nettle and not a stinger. It makes a wonderful filler plant for borders and the pink flowers are constant entertainment for visiting bees – definitely a plant to hunt down and include if you can.

As well as the ornamental plants, the weeds are also working their magic. My body is almost locked into the crouch position and, although I have a perfectly good kneeler in the shed, I still regularly kneel in the borders unprotected. I will have no one to blame but myself if I spend my dotage with housemaid's knee and a stoop.

The beekeeper visited today to check on his troops. He explained that it would be a slow start for honey this year. We're not the only ones to have had a long, cold winter and without extra feed the bees might not have made it. I sympathise – I'm not sure I'd have made it without a few extra chocolate brownies from our local bakery. The bees were given a ready-made feed in autumn before the temperature dropped. You can make a syrup from granulated sugar and water (2:1), the beekeeper tells me, but this is more work for the bees to process. Intrigued by exactly how the bees are fed, I asked the question. It always entertains me talking to a suited beekeeper – dressed in a similar way to Buzz Lightyear from *Toy Story*, the only answer I expect is "To Infinity and Beyond!" The syrup is put in a rapid feeder on top of the crown board under the lid of the hive, or a small frame feeder inside the hive. If the hive feels light during winter, or especially in spring before the temperature rises, then he will also give them a sugar fondant to stop them starving. This confirms that there is more to beekeeping than I've ever considered.

Friday 20th April

Yesterday I spread farmyard manure around the roses. Gardening and farming hand-in-hand has its advantages!

There's no shortage of appropriate poop in the countryside, of course, but it's getting it to your home that's usually the tricky part if you're not blessed with a farm next door. Farmyard manure is easy to come by, but you'll rarely find a farmer who has the time to drop off a small load to your home at this time of year. It's all go for them, with lambs coming thick and fast.

You could stop and buy sacks of fresh horse manure from the roadside. This is a great little pocket-money earner if you own a pony (I used to do it as a child). Those who source it this way will have to leave the manure to rest in the garden for a year before spreading. The manure I spread has been waiting in the field for well over a year now. Never be tempted to apply a fresh muck or you risk adding weed seed to your garden, and the concentration will be too rich and scorch the plants. Leave it to sit and the heat of the mound as it rots will kill off most weed seeds and mature nicely. Wait until there is plenty of worm activity in the heap and it smells particularly ripe.

Tuesday 24th April

Every year, around this time, I'm astounded by how many people haven't started to lavish time on their garden yet. Yes, this year has been a cold winter, but we are racing towards summer at an Olympic pace.

To cheer us onwards, the pear blossom is out. This arrives before the dessert apple and cider apple blossom. If you're clever with your planting, you can enjoy a relay of blossom from fruit trees right through until the end of May. If I had to choose one tree to grow for blossom it would be *Malus transitoria*. This crab apple grows tiny fruits that only the birds will find use for, but its blossom is out of this world.

The anemones are still flowering away in the garden. *Anemone nemorosa* 'Westwell Pink' has now turned from its original white to a shocking pink, which is rather fun. The prize for zingy colour, however, goes to one of my favourite plants,

APRIL

Smyrnium perfoliatum. This biennial could easily be mistaken for a euphorbia. It has lime-green foliage that really pops in the border. It will continue to share its joyful colour for weeks. After flowering it produces small, hard black seeds. In September, I pull up the plants and shake the seed over the border where I want it to grow. Simple. You'll rarely find this plant in a garden centre as it hates being in a pot, so look out for the seed in autumn and sow direct. In the first year the seedlings look like parsley, so don't weed them out. In the second year they put on the show. Do not be tempted to listen to those who say it is invasive – it can be but it's so simple to pull up that it is never a problem plant (well, this is my experience).

Talking of seed, I've sown some pink cosmos this week in seed trays. Cosmos is the perfect filler plant for gaps in borders later in the year. A gap in July is a real pain, as all that is left in the way of bedding plants at garden centres can be a little ropey by then. So, be prepared and sow cosmos or even better *Nicotiana* 'Lime Green'. Both are ideal for the middle or front of a border. The cosmos will flower right into October.

This year I've started to be more organised with my seed. I now have a seed tin in the kitchen filled with all the free seed I get with the numerous gardening magazines I buy. It's quickly turned into a treasure trove of possibility. It's tempting to pull out a packet of seed and sow the entire contents. My advice would be to sow about twenty per cent more than you need and no more. Otherwise if you don't have a greenhouse you'll be dancing around the seed trays in the spare room and getting across to the other side will be as tricky as a game of Twister after a glass of wine!

Wednesday 25th April

Today we've had hail, rain and sunshine – at last, a typical April has arrived. The garden looks quite incredible. Everything is so green and hopeful.

However, with the beauty comes a few beasts. By this, I mean dandelions. They have started to flower with gusto and there was I thinking I had pulled them all out. I comfort myself that some of our visitors may feel more at ease when they spot this familiar weed – even the 'professional' garden suffers from it. If you're a keen forager, perhaps you might not be so annoyed to see the dandelions. Their flowers can be eaten – I once dished them up as a starter for the family. Let's just say that they are an acquired taste.

The blossom on the edible pears has been quickly joined by that of *Prunus padus* (also known as bird cherry), the Asian pear and the ornamental silver pear (*Pyrus salicifolia* 'Pendula'). You can just about see a glimpse of pink blossom on our dessert apples. The only downside of blossom is that it falls, and you are left with the decision of whether to sweep it up – at least I have a very good dustpan! The light confetti on the grass is pretty, but after a while it will turn brown and start to look like litter. So I am leaving it for now, but it will soon end up on the compost heap. So many of April's delights are fleeting.

Today I spotted the bloodroot (*Sanguinaria canadensis*). It's the only species in the genus *Sanguinaria*, which makes it easy to remember. The sap in its rhizomes is blood-red and poisonous – how wonderfully ghoulish. Its flowers only tend to last for about a week, so I'm thrilled that I haven't let it pass without the chance to stand over it and coo. Another fleeting pleasure is the camassia. Its spires of blue flowers are over too quickly but maybe that is what makes us love them so much. They are often the star at the RHS Chelsea Flower Show in May, but I'm convinced that they need to mingle with other plants for success, rather than be planted in a solid drift as you might see in a show garden. No one wants to look at faded foliage after the flowers are over. As camassias are bulbs, you must leave the foliage on the plant to go yellow so that the energy can be reabsorbed for the following year. Foliage needs to be free to yellow in the sun. If you like the sound of a camassia in your own plot then plant bulbs in autumn in a sheltered, sunny spot in well-drained soil and mix them in with other perennials.

Don't you just hate reading that a plant needs a well-drained soil? You will have a job to find a plant that doesn't.

Things to do

- *Visit a bluebell wood.*
- *Divide hostas as they come into growth.*
- *Put well-rotted manure around your roses.*
- *At the end of the month sow hardy annuals outside.*
- *Clean out your vases. There's plenty of spring flowers to pick, and soft pussy willow makes a wonderful arrangement if you can find some.*
- *Keep a watchful eye out for nesting birds. It's at this time of year that you're likely to find a robin nesting in a compost bag. If you do, leave well alone.*
- *Pinch out the growing tips on sweet peas to encourage a bushy plant.*

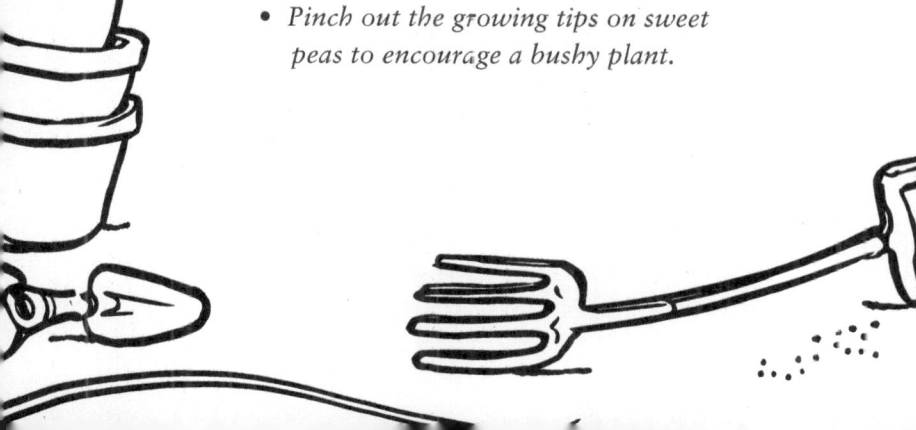

APRIL

Country Project

KEEPING HENS AND POULTRY

I grew up surrounded by feathers and fresh eggs. My mother collected poultry. Guinea fowl, quail, geese, ducks and hens were a huge part of my childhood.

If you keep poultry, free-range eggs are plentiful. Easter was a very important time for my family when my grandmother was alive, and eggs, as symbols of new life, were everywhere. She would get my sisters and I involved with creating the Easter garden in the church, and her Easter cake baked with freshly collected eggs was the highlight of the celebration. In its centre she would cut out a small circle of sponge and drop in an egg cup full of spring blooms such as primroses and violets. Far easier than fiddling about with icing sugar decorations! For high tea we would often have baked eggs: a spoonful of Marmite in the bottom of a mini ovenproof pot with an egg over the top, baked and eaten hot – delicious! I collected egg cups as a child and at one point I had over 150. No doubt the presence of chickens in the garden had something to do with the inspiration for starting my collection. A free-range, garden-laid egg is like nothing else.

However, as with many country pursuits, keeping poultry is not without its disadvantages and drawbacks, so before you fill your garden with chickens, there are some practical considerations to take into account. I must admit I do get frustrated with those who think it would be fun to have a few hens without the slightest bit of knowledge about the realities of keeping them – you need to be well prepared for life with feathered friends.

How to keep hens

The next few paragraphs might seem a little negative, but it's best to be ready for life with poultry. I don't want to squash your dreams but you might as well know the facts before you start.

1. You'll need more space than you think. Hens in the garden are extremely worthwhile, but if you have a small plot and plan to create just one run for them, it won't work. At first you'll be thrilled with the pleasure that your feathered friends bring. They'll be happily scratching about in their new home, enjoying the worms, grass and weeds. This is the calm before the storm! After a month or less the run will become a compacted, rather boring pen of soil peppered with giant chicken poos and dustbowls created by the birds. You won't be able to reseed it or regenerate it unless you have a second run on standby.

2. Free-range means free to eat anything in the garden. If keeping hens in a run is not for you then why not let them freely roam? I adore this method of keeping chickens as they add another dimension to the plot – fear! The garden will never be uneventful whatever time of the year as you will have to guard your precious seedlings or they'll be scratched up. You also have the added fear that a fox will come and feast, so you must train your hens to go to bed in a foxproof house every evening or you'll soon lose them.

3. Rats and other annoyances. Rats and chickens go hand in hand, and it's for this reason that I don't keep them anymore. Mites are also an issue unless, like my mother, you are prepared to clean the henhouse very regularly and apply mite powder to unwilling victims. I have often seen my mother emerge from a henhouse in a boilersuit covered in feathers!

4. Best breeds. Marans give wonderful brown eggs but I prefer the common or garden brown hen, the Golden Comet, as they're very friendly. For looks, nothing much can beat the giant and rather flamboyant Orpingtons, although they don't lay that many eggs.

5. You really don't need a cockerel. Unless you want to breed chicks, your hens will lay and be very happy – sometimes happier – without one!

Must-have plants

Alchemilla mollis
Alliums
Ammi majus
Anthriscus sylvestris 'Ravenswing'
Astrantia
Hardy geraniums
Irises
Peonies
Tulipa sprengeri
Wisteria

MAY

I have returned unscathed
from the city!

Tool Kit

RHS Chelsea Flower Show tickets. If you can't get to Chelsea, go to one of the RHS regional shows. They are held throughout the year.

Red nail polish to disguise muddy nails when you go out into society!

A list of local gardens you plan to visit.

String, plant ties and plant supports.

A good pair of cut-flower scissors, a gardening trug and a wide-brimmed hat for sunny days.

Plenty of pots and baskets for bedding plants, and slow-release plant feed.

A comfy garden chair to admire the view.

May

My feet don't touch the ground in May. The rewards for winter work are coming in thick and fast and even those with a passing interest in plants are tempted to peep over garden walls.

If your heart isn't filled with joy now, you've got your eyes closed. We are surrounded by beauty in the countryside and the city has lots to offer this month too.

Anyone involved in gardens and gardening will be busy and buzzing with excitement – it's all happening. RHS Chelsea is the highlight of May for many gardeners, and on the farm, shearing is a priority. The yards where the cattle have lived all winter are cleared out and muck is stacked and left ready to be spread in the autumn after harvest. I'll be raking some of this steaming pile onto the veg patch later in the year. It's wonderful to see the cattle in the fields again enjoying the emerald green grass.

Thursday 3rd May

We have a small nursery in our local market town that sells bedding plants almost exclusively. The nursery is just by a set of very busy traffic lights and waiting for the lights to change gives me time to eye up the goods.

Today I pulled in – the array of colourful annuals was too tempting. As a result, the afternoon was spent putting out the bedding. It's still a risk, as last week the cardiocrinums (Himalayan lilies) were hit by frost. However, you get to a point where you can't wait any longer and empty pots look pitiful. I'm still wearing a scarf to garden and it stays on in the evening in my unheated home. The family told me that buying an old, listed property with flagstone floors was a mistake, but I refused to hear sense. I don't regret it for a moment, and I am hoping that the experience will be character-building for my young son. I'm sure that one day he will look back and smile at the thought of his mother going to bed in a bobble hat!

The garden changes every day – only a fool would leave their garden at this time of year. The tall stems of the nectaroscordums are leaping from borders like snakes being charmed and the camassias are perfection. Changes are fast and being absent for even a couple of days means you miss out on the action.

The tulips are fully open, which saddens me. Although they look splendid in full flounce, I adore them when they are tight in bud and I can't bear the thought of the petals falling. Tulips are so fleeting but so fabulous. Last autumn I discovered *Tulipa* 'Brown Sugar' and it's now in flower. What a perfect name for this sweet orange delight. Tulips rarely perform well for more than one year so we plant fresh bulbs in large terracotta pots every year at Stockton Bury. Once the flowers have faded, the pots can be swiftly removed to allow the tulips to die disgracefully out of sight. The old bulbs are either planted into my mother's garden, where they will put on a very hotchpotch display and are cut for church flowers, or they are thrown out. This may seem frivolous, but it is the only way to ensure a crisp and attention-grabbing display for paying guests.

Blossom is plentiful in the garden this month, with *Prunus padus* 'Colorata' my favourite this week. Although the *Staphylea colchica* is looking fabulous, dripping with chains of white blooms, I still hold a candle for good old-fashioned apple blossom and it's just about to put on a show.

Friday 4th May

Today I decided to tackle a rather embarrassing clump of nettles. I launched myself at this project with force. However, despite wearing gloves, I've been left with very stung arms and the first insect bite of the year.

I'm not sure if the culprit was a bee or something else but my arm feels heavy and sore. My beekeeper friend tells me that drinking wine, eating bananas and wearing perfume will attract bees to sting you. I'll have to give up supping wine as I weed! As for perfume – what's that? Gardeners don't tend to tart themselves up to tend the tulips. If you invade the space of a honeybee, remain calm is the advice. I tried this last summer when one landed on my head. The noise of a buzzing bee is quite overwhelming. As I stood still, with a look of fear, my uncle approached and shouted, "Bee!" as he batted my head. This sent both the bee and me into overdrive; the result was a sting above the eye, a very swollen forehead and, alas, a dead bee. I'm yet to decide if the bump was from the bee sting or being clocked over the head by my uncle. This gardening lark can be very dangerous.

Monday 7th May

Wow, it's hot today. Watering potted plants is the first job, to help the plants stand up to the weather. I get it done early, because midday watering can lead to scorch and loss of moisture through evaporation ... and that's just what happens to me after lifting can after can of water.

I've also taken the seedlings out of the steaming hot polytunnel and put them outside in the shade. My task now is to remove all traces of dandelion from the garden. They are in full flower at this time of year and if you leave them even one more day you will have seed floating everywhere. I challenged myself to make it all the way around the garden without getting sidetracked – dandelions only today! I have a terrible habit of moving from one area of the garden to another. I wish I was one of those people who could focus. I'm a Gemini – that's my excuse.

As I weed, I note the huge change in the plants this week. The leaves of the snowdrops have turned yellow and are starting to look a mess – I'll pull the foliage off next week (see above: mustn't get sidetracked). The fritillaries have now faded but as they do so they put on an impressive growth spurt of about 10cm, so that they can successfully throw their seeds about – ingenious. I spot the first tree peony today, which means that in a week's time we will have high winds and heavy rain. These short-lived flowers always seem to be hit by the weather when they are at their most impressive. Camassias are still in flower but this heat won't help with their endurance, and the first of the flower buds on the *Tulipa sprengeri* are visible. Bluebells are stunning today and, by the ponds, *Caltha palustris* (marsh marigold) must be the plant of the week. It's simply gorgeous.

Today is the first day of the year that I'm gardening in flip flops. I don't recommend this, especially if using sharp tools! My neatly painted red toes now have mud between them, but who cares? My jeans are rolled up to my knees; the thought of shorts is just taking it all too far. You won't ever see my legs on show. They are so far beyond white, I think they are, in fact, blue.

Most gardeners today must at last be feeling that summer is here. More bedding plants are going out and I'm putting in the sweet peas. This is the kind of day that you want to walk across the lawn barefoot, or just lie on the grass and watch the clouds rolling by. But alas, it is not to be for me today. I must rescue a bird trapped in the outside toilet. Was he hiding from the heat of the sun or from me?

Thursday 10th May

I've spent the morning crouching under a beech hedge. I'm convinced I will get stuck in this position at some point this summer. I'm fortunate to have a good back but there's been a temporary glitch – not due to gardening but thanks to a poor decision to play football with my son wearing steel toe-capped boots.

MAY

I'm not hiding from garden visitors under this hedge; I'm simply clearing the last of the brown and crispy leaves. It seems very odd to be pushing a barrow of leaves on a sunny May day. A beech hedge is a joy but it clings tightly to its foliage and continues to drop leaves weeks after all the other trees and shrubs have given up.

I almost can't keep up with the constant change in the garden this week. The pear blossom is now finished; it was overtaken by the blossom in the cider orchard, which is just about to put on the most incredible show. The wisteria that's planted on the sheltered south-facing wall is streaks ahead of the other wisterias thanks to the extra heat it enjoys. Borders are luscious and green and have yet to have their foliage damaged or marked by the scorching heat of summer. It looks like it will be a fantastic year for the martagon lilies; I only hope the dashing red lily beetle doesn't take a fancy to them. Tree peonies are just about to put on an oversized display, but the most exciting development of the week is the growth on *Cardiocrinum giganteum*. These giant Himalayan lilies have impressive heart-shaped leaves and, after about five to seven years, they produce a huge flower stem that carries oversized white trumpet flowers. After they've flowered they die – but don't despair! Babies appear at the base of the plant to take on the show in future years.

As well as the traditional May blooms there are a few plants in the garden in flower now that seem more suited to the pallet of August. The sophora, with its claw-like bright yellow flower, and the equally yellow *Petteria ramentacea*, have the look of midsummer. For me, May is the month for blues, purples and pinks; and bluebells, alliums, camassias and blossoms suit the mood.

Sunday 13th May

Today was the perfect day to slowly wander down a country lane, admiring the wild flowers. The light breeze was full of dandelion fluff. It was almost raining seed. Despite my efforts at weeding, I'm predicted a huge crop of yellow flowers in the garden next year!

As I was moving sheep today I fell away from my fellow shepherds and meandered along, looking at the hedgerows. Cow parsley is at waist height and under its wiry stems are compact displays of herb robert and greater stitchwort. My only hope is that the verges aren't trimmed too hastily, as this is heaven. As a child, before I knew that picking wildflowers was a sin, I would make a trail of cow parsley to mark my route around the country lanes. As I plodded along on my dumpy pony, I would grab fistfuls of it and drop the flowers and stems on the road. This was before the era of mobile phones; I knew that if I got lost, I could simply follow my flowery route home. Cow parsley is by far and away my most treasured plant.

It's been a busy week in the garden. The sweet peas are now planted under the hazel twigs that were coppiced in February and the bedding plants are all in. I've been sowing seed direct into terracotta pans, which have germinated well, but today I spotted that slugs have harvested half of my seedlings. Disaster. Visitors have been in high spirits this week. I'd like to have kept one particular lady. She was on a coach holiday and arrived in her gardening clothes. Her body warmer was well-worn and muddy; she didn't care a jot. She was full of life, despite being in her eighties, and her energy was infectious. I hope I'm half as buoyant when I reach her age. Another couple announced they had been married for 50 years. "It's worked well for us," the lady explained, as she clutched a basket of plants to buy. "He earns the money and I spend it."

Wednesday 16th May

All the best plants are fleeting. I opened my front door this morning to see that the wind had taken my last tulip petals and the path was covered in what I am calling blitter (blossom litter).

We now face the decision of whether to sweep up the blitter or leave it. Most visitors to the garden are not offended by a confetti of fresh petals on the paths but as it turns brown it's a different story. I suspect I shall have to crack out the broom.

On my morning drive to drop my son at school I noticed that the buttercups have joined us. Although I'm almost insulted by the presence of a dandelion in my borders, I'm quite happy to welcome the odd buttercup to the party. Their shiny petals reflect light so well that, as we all know, they are used for the obligatory test under the chin to check if you like butter. They also remind me of my late father, who died when buttercups were in full bloom. When I pass from this world, please let it be in a pretty month and not when winter is blasting at the windows.

In the garden, strawberries are in flower and the pompoms of the viburnums have transformed from green into whites or pinks. Camassias are just about hanging on in there and I've been on a mission to discover the name of a dark purple camassia that has been growing here for a couple of years. According to my

Twitter friends it might be 'Maybelle'. I wonder what gardeners of yesteryear would think of tweeters. I'm no social media obsessive but I have to confess that it has helped me identify many plants and pests that might otherwise escape me. Facebook too has been invaluable this year for promoting events in the garden. I know I need to embrace this new way of communicating with gardeners or no one will know that Stockton Bury exists – I keep reminding myself that this is progress and progress is good. Gardeners need to share experiences to succeed so I must move with the times.

Friday 18th May

One of my favourite places on earth is the Great Pavilion at RHS Chelsea Flower Show. Next week, the gates to this incredible horticultural spectacle will be opened to the public.

I'm one of the lucky ones who will be seeing the show before ticket-holders get the chance. I've not been welcomed into the royal family but it's the next best thing: this is my first year as a judge. On Saturday afternoon, my job is to look around the gardens prior to the judging day on Sunday. As it's still build-up, and construction will be ongoing, we are instructed to wear steel toe-capped boots. That's all well and good, but this morning my boots are messier than they have ever been. They've just been worn to shift a pile of well-rotted manure and now they're about to hit the glittering city streets of London. Typical.

When you're gardening on your own most days, you don't tend to look in the mirror very often. However, this trip has led me to focus on my appearance for a snap second. Wow, I've gone grey. I thought gardening was meant to relax you and delay the signs of ageing? I wonder if I'm alone in being concerned about my appearance? Will famous TV gardeners also be all a-flutter this week about their outfits? As I inspect my nails I see that they are full of soil. I'll need to paint them this evening. You may think it odd for a gardener to paint their nails but, trust me, it's the only way to make them half respectable!

Before I leave the cosy confides of the Herefordshire countryside for the bright lights of the city, I want to write down the dramatic changes in the scenery here at Stockton Bury. The tree peonies and wisteria are still leading the show, but these will soon be joined by *Tulipa sprengeri*. This tiny little species tulip litters the borders here after years of self-seeding. Few gardeners seem to have success with these, but even though each bulb is a pretty penny they're worth a go, as our display attests. Plant them deep; this should prevent them becoming a feast for mice. The vegetable patch is looking immaculate at the moment, with neat rows of seedlings offering that regimented look that I adore. Starting your career as a parks gardener and greenkeeper leaves you with an affection for bare soil and straight lines. Far less orderly are the buttercups sparkling in the surrounding fields, but I forgive them. The yellow of the oilseed rape is slowly fading but hayfever season is still with us.

After sorting my nails, my next mission is to choose an outfit for the show. One thing is for sure it won't be a dress. My knees have certainly seen better days.

Tuesday 22nd May

I have returned unscathed from the city! The last few days have been just like a dream.

MAY

Rubbing shoulders with the great and the good of the gardening world can lead you to question your right to be alongside them. I remind myself that all the hours of weeding and watching plants germinate, grow and die must entitle me to a little bit of glitz.

RHS Chelsea is not just about the glamour, however. The true highlights aren't watching celebrities strike a pose in front of the petunias or listening to the guffaws of laughter from amongst the lupins – the plants own the show. At Chelsea I watched in wonder as an army of bees razzle-dazzled amongst the roses and considered what they would think when this convenient sweetshop of nectar disappears at the end of the week. The bees will probably feel as I do now, after spending a few days surrounded by nature's sweetness: exhausted, elated and at the same time bereft.

Judging is an honour and something that I take far more seriously than anything else I have ever done. I was moved so much by one particular garden that I had a job not to shed a tear. Ignore all those grumps who tell you not to visit this show as it's too crowded and the gardens are all too modern and expensive. Those people just don't get it. RHS Chelsea Flower Show should be on everyone's bucket list.

As I walked the pavements of gold in Kensington in my steel toecaps, for a moment I considered a life as a city-dweller. Constant, reliable wifi; fabulous cafes and posh restaurants; swanky cars. But here, sitting at my wobbly kitchen table with the garden door flung open and birdsong drifting in, I know that this is definitely home.

Monday 28th May

It's the calm after the storm. Yesterday the garden was home to our plant fair with fifteen local nurseries and garden suppliers attending and it was my job to make it a successful day.

The evening before the event the night sky was alive with thunder and lightning. Did I sleep? No! I really should know by now that a gardener might have some chance of controlling a garden but there is certainly no way of influencing the weather. It will be what it will be. No amount of praying and worrying will change it. I should also know by now that real gardeners will come to buy plants whatever the weather.

The day before I had attempted to make the entrance of the garden a floral delight with cut cow parsley, ragged robin, *Alchemilla mollis* and, for foliage, young shoots of beech and laurel. It's easy to make a good-looking arrangement when you garden in the countryside. For early summer garden parties, simply fill your window boxes with flower arrangements in jam jars instead of presenting your guests with a few immature bedding plants. Avoid buying florists' foam as it's non-biodegradable; a ball of chicken wire works just as well, but you'll need to have the flower stems in water. However, if you already have florist foam it's most eco-friendly to reuse it rather than throw it away. A word of caution. My attempt to make a ball of cow parsley initially failed! Don't try to hang a soaked foam ball with garden wire – it will drop to the floor like a head that's been severed by a guillotine. Put the foam in a net first and then hang that.

Looking around, I can tell that the garden is just about to enter a transition period. Thanks to the heavy rain the wisteria is past its best and next week the flowers will hang like wet socks on a washing line. The wonderful display that *Clematis montana* 'Elizabeth' offers has faded and the tree peonies will do well to cling to their last petals. Ribbons of *Tulipa sprengeri* have the trump card this week. Candelabra primulas light up the edges of the stream and the honeysuckle is perfection. My favourite *Cornus*, 'Eddie's White Wonder', is past its best but my second favourite, the subtler pink *Cornus* 'Satomi', is certainly at its peak.

Under the south-facing wall, the foliage of the boisterous *Inula racemosa* adds a tropical touch, but the incredible spires of the pale pink flowers of *Dictamnus albus* var. *purpureus* are the show-stopper. The borders are now home to perfect spheres of allium flowers, towers of lupins, clumps of hardy geraniums and the odd giant poppy, everything cushioned by a generous duvet of green foliage.

Thursday 31st May

I've escaped. I know I wrote earlier that only fools leave their garden in May but if I don't exit my countryside plot occasionally I'm in danger of forgetting what lies beyond the hedges. Surely you'll let me off as we are nearly entering June.

Today I visited another open garden, partly for pleasure but mostly to see how they do it. This is my idea of heaven – my husband is less impressed. He remained in the car for a sleep as my son and I headed eagerly for the entrance. After many years, I have at last got over the fact that not everyone enjoys a garden, although I do feel sad for those who don't see beauty in plants or yearn to be submerged in natural gorgeousness. Perhaps I should be grateful that my husband doesn't have an eye for beauty, or he certainly wouldn't have married me. He has generously given me the nickname of 'worm', so at least he has drawn on the garden for his inspiration in one way.

As we walk through the woodland garden, my twelve-year-old says "Lovely hostas". We are both shocked! He knows a plant name, and not just one – he went on to identify an iris. Hours of standing over me in the garden, begging me to hurry up and come inside, have led to him absorbing some gardening knowledge. This is a miracle. Maybe in the future, when his partner wants to enjoy a garden visit, he won't choose to stay in the car and sleep.

This moment of brilliance reminds me of another time he 'identified' a plant. As a ten-year-old he appeared behind me as I was talking to a visitor in the garden. They were showing me a photograph on their mobile phone and asking for a plant to be identified. As I scratched my head, a little voice from behind me said, "It's a hysterectomy." Where on earth had he heard that word? He was convinced that it was a plant name!

On the way back from our garden-visiting adventure we pulled into a layby to have a snack. My mobile rang. "Good afternoon," said a lady. "About five years ago I bought a plant from you and I want you to tell me the name of it, because I can't remember. It has green leaves and white flowers," she told me. I waited, patiently, but it turned out that was the full extent of the description. I might like my plants but please, if you're looking for an identification, give the gardener more! Height, time of year it flowers, scent, size of flower... I'm afraid on this occasion I could not assist.

Things to do

- *Harden off dahlias, but wait until all danger of frost has passed before you plant them out.*

- *Plant sweet peas out if the weather looks to remain mild.*

- *Keep an eye out for lily beetles. These dashing red beetles fall on their back as soon as you reach out to pick them off. If you find them, squish them.*

- *Cut back daffodils and tulips only once the foliage has turned yellow.*

- *Mow your lawn in a different direction each week (and run across it barefoot for the first time this summer to dip your toes in the pond!).*

- *Clip box and yew hedges but check for birds nests first.*

Country Project

GROWING FLOWERS FOR CUTTING

There's something rather wonderful about wandering down the garden with a Sussex trug to pick flowers. And there's something even more wonderful about having flowers in the house that haven't racked up any air-miles or cost you a pretty packet.

I adore cutting flowers but tend to do this at my own home. Although we don't cut flowers from the borders at Stockton Bury, my grandmother was permitted to cut just one giant dahlia a week for the centre of the table. It would be presented in a small, traditional bowl (which always made me think of goldfish) and on occasion earwigs would wander out of the flower and cause us to giggle.

May is the only month that I would dare to offer to do someone's wedding flowers. Frothy displays of cow parsley, *Alchemilla mollis* and astrantia, joined by a few roses, is as romantic as you can get. But it's not just this month that offers delights: you can have cut flowers all summer long if you plan your patch with care.

When you go to the effort of growing and picking your own flowers, make sure you show them off to their best advantage. Place your vase in a cool place. My ancient rural beamed idyll with flagstone floors is cold so I can keep a vase of flowers going for weeks even in summer – the thought of this in the depths of winter gives me slight comfort as I hobble around the house with chilblains!

How to have a cutting garden

If you're keen to have a vase of flowers on the table all summer, then it's worth planning and planting a dedicated cutting garden.

1. Plan your patch. Choose a relatively sheltered spot, that gets a lot of sun. Planting in rows makes weeding and supporting your plants easier – give yourself room to walk up and down the rows to pick.

2. Think creatively. If you don't have a dedicated spot to grow rows and rows of flowers to cut, sweet peas, gladioli and dahlias can all work well in a kitchen garden, and borders and herb gardens can all offer opportunities for brightly coloured bulbs and perennials with a long picking season and shrubs with interesting foliage.

3. Choose your favourites. Grow what you love. I'm a fan of *Ammi majus* (an alternative to cow parsley), cornflowers, cosmos and zinnias.

4. Pay attention when picking. First thing in the morning, when flowers have been perked up after being refreshed by the moisture of the night, is a good time to cut.

SEASONAL TREATS

February

There's still a few Brussels sprouts on offer in the garden and the tops are worth picking to add to a stir fry. Parsnips are coming to an end: they're tough now, but boil and mash them and no one will know. It's still a little early to start foraging in the countryside so we eat from the freezer. My uncle lives off frozen fruits this month. Lift the lid of the chest freezer here and you'll find what looks like a blood bank. It's bags of stewed damsons collected from the hedgerows in late September. They are yummy served with ice cream or poured over your cereal (look out for the pips, though). If you are tempted to forage, you might find the odd *Viola odorata* in the garden (the flowers are edible) and some dandelions. However, having eaten fried dandelion flowers, I really would not recommend them unless you find yourself unexpectedly on an adventure with Bear Grylls.

March

There are plenty of leeks to have with the Sunday roast, but my sister's chickens are enjoying the last of the sprout tops – we're all sick of them now. If you've got your own hens, expect a few more eggs this month. Eggs don't come with a date stamp, so invest in an egg rack with a few layers. Rotate them so everyone in the family knows which ones need eating first – oldest eggs on the top! Poached eggs on a bed of freshly picked, lightly wilted spinach and sprinkled with cracked black pepper makes a yummy lunchtime meal. The cellar here is still home to our stores of cooking apples. A wonderfully warming treat is a baked apple with mincemeat in the centre, but if, like me, you're not a fan of raisins, a sprinkling of brown sugar is an acceptable alternative.

April

British lamb is just appearing in the shops and, as far as I'm concerned, it simply must be eaten with homemade mint sauce and a thick onion or leek sauce. Purple sprouting broccoli, which was sown in June last year, is usually ripe for picking if the pigeons haven't got there first. This is the month to make nettle soup, because the fresh young growth is much tastier. Nettles have a taste like spinach; don't write it off until you've tried it. And, of course, if Easter falls in this month, chocolate is very much in season with little clusters of chocolate eggs to discover in many gardens at this time. The Easter Bunny is more than welcome in my garden – all other bunnies are not permitted.

May

The highlight of May for me and many others is the appearance of asparagus spears. They might take a few years to produce, and take up space, but wow – a spear dripping in butter is so worth it. Herb gardens are springing into life and it's a good time to buy extra herbs for containers and beds. Early sowers will be enjoying their first salad crops, and my son will have to perfect the art of removing lettuce from his plate without me noticing all over again. Rhubarb is also cropping and a great dinner party dessert is to stew it with a sprinkling of brown sugar to taste. Just before you take the fruit off the gentle heat, add a splash of Amaretto. While the rhubarb is cooling, place a layer of Madeira cake in the bottom of a wine glass (one for each guest). Then spoon over the rhubarb when cool, add a dollop of whisked cream and sprinkle with grated or flaked chocolate. Even people who claim not to like rhubarb will love this.

Must-have plants

Alstroemeria 'Indian Summer'
Cornus kousa 'Miss Satomi'
Dactylorhiza fuchsii
Gladiolus cardinalis
Hemerocallis 'Alan'
Laburnum anagyroides
Lilium martagon
Rosa 'Complicata'
Salvia nemorosa 'Caradonna'
Sanguisorba officinalis
Veratrum viride

JUNE

Anyone for tennis?

Tool Kit

Antihistamines and SPF50 sun cream
(with any luck you'll need it!).

Spare colander for daily fruit-picking, and an old
milking stool to sit on when picking gooseberries.

Cream to go with your freshly
picked strawberries.

A chest freezer to store excess fruits –
raspberries freeze particularly well.

Tomato feed.

A good salad spinner – you'll be having
lettuce most days from now on.

A magnifying glass and a good insect
identification book.

June

Visitors flock to open gardens to sit back and smell the roses. It's peak season and your garden should be looking its Sunday best.

However stunning your plot is, I've learnt that at the end of the month to expect a downturn in visitor numbers if you run an open garden. It seems that most garden lovers are quick to abandon a visit in exchange for tennis – yes, even the best roses can't compete with the appeal of watching Novak Djokovic and Rafael Nadal at Wimbledon. We might be a nation of garden lovers, but sport is a healthy competitor for our attention. Don't even get me started on the cricket!

It's also a month to worry about the weather – but then, gardeners are often accused of talking about nothing else all year round. Farmers are just as guilty in June as they pray for sunshine in order to cut their hay and silage. A heavy rain shower this month can cause untold damage to a border, especially if it's coupled with strong winds. Perennials that once stood tall will need propping up. I often wonder what will greet me when I take my morning walk around the garden. Will there be casualties?

Friday 8th June

Last night the rain came down with some force so today is perfect for planting out. The ground is soft and moist and I'm putting annual cosmos and eschscholzia plants into the borders.

The disadvantage of heavy summer rain is that it looks as if the perennials have had a falling out overnight. They're lolling all over the place as if they're injured, and some are off their legs completely. Colette and I set to work in haste this morning to save the wounded before the garden opened. With a wheelbarrow each, packed with plant supports of all different shapes and sizes, we were the Emergency First Aid team carrying stretchers and crutches.

Supporting plants on your own is tricky – it's far easier with a friend. One holds the plant back and the other puts in the support. Don't do what we did and get the person without the waterproof to hold the plant back; they'll end up soaked to the skin. Secretly, I like to brush past foliage; I adore the feeling of walking through what looks like an untravelled track, but with borders so packed with plants, here at Stockton Bury we cut back or prop up anything bending over the narrow paths to prevent visitors from crushing the lush foliage or tripping over stems.

You may wonder why I haven't already supported everything in the garden ahead of a summer storm. I was wondering the same thing this morning. However, in my defence, some years you can get away without any supports at all in a sheltered garden. I have known gardens where supports are put out in very early summer. This is, of course, sensible: you avoid the trussed-up look that results in leaving it too late. Plants look so much more

JUNE

natural using a support if they have chosen their own route up it. The garden at Stockton Bury is sheltered, so wind is not usually a problem. We've just been unlucky today. It's up to you to decide how vulnerable your garden is – as with many things in gardening, there's no one-size-fits-all solution.

The rain overnight has turned the fields that surround the garden to emerald green. The grass is lush and knee-high; so long that you could easily lose your sheep in it. Most have been sheared by now and are feeling the relief of being freed of their heavy wool coats. In wet conditions such as this I made my first visit to Great Dixter in East Sussex, the home of the late Christopher Lloyd. The rain was biblical but, having driven so far, I was not going to be put off. Many people let even the slightest suggestion of inclement weather put them off a garden visit – but not me. In fact, my time there couldn't have been better. The appearance of rain clouds also meant the quick disappearance of fellow visitors, seeking shelter. I found myself gloriously alone in that magical and usually busy place.

Back here at Stockton Bury, baptisias are outstanding this week; they're so content in the clay soil that they've reached waist height. Poppies are plentiful and the fleeting lupins are beginning to go over. Thanks to this wet and warm weather the cardiocrinums are starting to show their buds and the foxgloves and martagon lilies are out of this world. The roses are nearly at their best, with *Rosa* 'Wollerton Old Hall' one of my favourites thanks to its scent. I've found that as you start to get older you have a sudden, deep appreciation for the scent of roses.

Crops in the kitchen garden are behaving as if they're on rocket fuel – this is such good growing weather. I do have some bad news amongst this glorious riot of floriferous activity, however. After a very long and cold winter, many pests and diseases have been lying low. I certainly haven't seen many slugs and snails about these parts – they're hiding themselves well! Now all that has suddenly changed. Black spot is emerging on the roses and we have hundreds of caterpillars of the ermine moth wiggling around in sticky hammocks in our apple trees. This is a disaster, and rather scary, if I'm honest. Will they take over? It looks like they might. There will be very few apples as a result this year but the trees should bounce back the following year.

My automatic answer to pests and diseases is either to run for the hills (unhelpful) or cut out the stems and leaves affected. I started pulling off sticky nets of cobwebs of the apple ermine moth, but soon realised I was on a hiding to nothing. I know I have weeks ahead of garden visitors reporting it to me at the end of their visit, "Did you know that you have a problem with your fruit trees?"

In fact, my go-to place for pest and disease advice is the comprehensive RHS website. Here you'll find both non-pesticide and pesticide control treatments. Identify your troubles quickly and try to react before the problem gets worse – a little like you might with a verruca.

Monday 11th June

It's my birthday and one thing is for sure – my uncle will present me with my annual Tupperware box of lamb's liver. Yes, liver! It's my favourite.

June is a fantastic month to be born. If everyone forgets about my day (apart from Uncle and the liver) I can quite easily pick myself a bunch of flowers from the garden. When picking flowers over the last few weeks I would always include cow parsley, my favourite, but now that it's over, it can be replaced with the very similar flowers of the ground elder. As much as I dread this weed, its flowers are rather pretty. There's no ground elder at Stockton Bury but plenty in my own garden a few miles away. Add some *Alchemilla mollis* and a few single roses and you have the perfect country bunch.

The year is racing by. When I look in the hedgerows I can see small blackberries forming. Can that really be happening already? Every evening I walk my Border terrier Larry and admire the verges and hedges – the real country garden. Fortunately, the local farmers here are as keen as I am to save the wildflowers that decorate the country lanes, and they hold off cutting the verges for as long as possible. If they didn't, we'd miss the giant leaves of the butterbur and the twinkling pink flowers of herb robert and ragged robin. I recently discovered that butterburr leaves were, fittingly, traditionally used to wrap butter. If you dig deep enough into the past, most wildflowers have been put to good use in the home.

This evening I'm going to attempt to make my first elderflower cordial. I have bags of caster sugar on the kitchen table at home and a basket at the ready to forage.

Thursday 14th June

The weather forecast predicted heavy rain and wind last night. The wind was enthusiastic, to say the least, so on arrival at the garden this morning the spherical heads of the viburnum were blowing around and the scene reminded me of an empty town centre the morning after New Year's Eve (it smelled a lot better, though).

JUNE

The past two days have been very busy in the garden – we are certainly in the high season of garden visiting. I must confess that by the end of the day I'm shattered; I often feel very much as if I've been on *Mastermind*. My chosen specialist subject is, "You've got a green plant – what is it?"

Today I managed to fathom out from a description what a visitor's mystery plant might be: *Calycanthus chinensis*. Pleased with myself, I told the lady the name. Then she asked – but what is it? To which I could only reply, "A plant." We all get confused with plant names: there's no shame in it. Some gardeners are obsessed with recording the varieties in their garden and others couldn't care less what they are called as long as they grow. I sit somewhere in the middle. To be honest, it is very hard to remember plants unless you have spent good money on them. Buy them, plant them and then the name should stick.

Campanulas are taking over here and today I've picked a sample of each and placed them in jars with a label. I'm hoping that by putting them on the kitchen windowsill I will learn them and be able to answer the inevitable questions when they come with a little more authority. In my little sample jars I have *Campanula glomerata* 'Superba' (surely I won't forget this one!) with its wonderful balls of flowers, and *C.* 'Sarastro' with electric blue flowers (a plant that's full of vigour). Flowering slightly later than these is *C. lactiflora* 'Alba', *C. lactiflora* 'Loddon Anna' and the stunning bell-shaped *C. persicifolia*. From experience, the hardest to accommodate in a garden are the *C. lactiflora* types, as they grow to such height and tend to need a great deal of support. Don't let that put you off, however: a plant that flowers for weeks on end in high summer is worth its weight in gold.

After propping up the wounded from last night's gusts, I spent time in The Dingle, Stockton Bury's water garden. The pond weed has certainly taken hold and tomorrow I will be armed with a fishing rod to scoop it out. The pond weed must be left by the pond for 24 hours so any displaced pond life can creep back to its watery home. Whilst surveying the water garden I was thrilled to spot some bright orange trollius and a few candelabra primulas looking very much at home. I can't help but lean in and pull the odd weed. Rosebay willowherb is now knee-high and in dire need of pulling before it flowers and sets seed.

The bearded iris are coming to an end but there is still plenty to admire today: *Calycanthus* x *raulstonii* 'Hartlage Wine' is a favourite with guests, along with baptisia and the slowly unfolding flowers of the veratrums. *Allium* 'Ambassador' is the most masterful of all the alliums this week with huge flowers on stems reaching 1.2m. They look like the lollipops from Roald Dahl's *Charlie and the Chocolate Factory* and the bees are all over them. Today was rounded off by putting the very first bunch of home-grown sweet peas in a milk bottle. Perfect.

Saturday 16th June

The countryside has changed dramatically this month. The flowers of the oilseed rape are over, but the plants have grown so much that it's almost impossible to walk the footpaths in fields planted with the crop. Wheat is knee-high already and the potatoes are sprouting with gusto along the clay soil ridges.

In the garden, climbers are reaching out from their supports like aliens on the hunt for human prey. Their twining stems stretch to tap you on the shoulder when you pass by. Vines, kiwi and wisteria are growing at speed. Wisteria is the most wonderful climber for a house if you have the patience. In late May your walls will drip with spectacular pink, blue or white racemes of scented flowers. Throw open the windows and the delicate perfume will drift in. Once the flowers fade, the plant puts its foot down and grows at a pace. The foliage creates a curtain across the windows that will keep your south-facing rooms cool and shaded – you'll no longer need net curtains for privacy.

If you fancy a new set of curtains for next summer, wait to buy your wisteria until next May. It's a plant that I would suggest you buy in flower. Invest in a non-flowering plant and you might be waiting for years and years to have a bloom. To train this giant up, use strong wires attached to the house not a piece of flimsy trellis. The trunk on the wisteria here is thicker than the top of my leg and it's only 40 years old (not my leg – the plant!) Your trellis will be eaten alive by this climber's strong and twisting stems.

I was entertained today by Colette. As we weeded under the shady branches of the *Paulownia* trees (foxglove tree) she came across a seed head. "What does this belong to?" she asked.

"It's the seed pod of the *Paulownia* that's way up above us," I replied.

With that she looked up, with a face filled with terror, and said, "I have made a stupid, stupid mistake."

It turns out that she has planted two of these big trees in her small garden. Offering little comfort other than a giggle I explained that the tree we were under was about 30 years old and it would take a while for her to be completely swamped by her plants at home. This does raise the issue, though, of choosing the right plant for the right place. It's impossible to plant a garden that will never need thinning. The planting at Stockton Bury is about 35 years old and the trees are largely at their maximum height. Some will soon have to be completely removed, and others crown lifted.

Without taking control of your top storey you will no longer need your mower, your sun hat or your plant supports. The garden beneath the canopy will disappear. Trees need to be controlled or you'll quickly lose your garden altogether.

Tuesday 19th June

For the wheels of the countryside to continue to turn we all must do our bit. You really shouldn't settle rurally without getting involved with some sort of charity or community work.

I've been judging private gardens for the local agricultural show. As the only judge for this section, the pressure was on to find three plots worthy of prizes. I met my fellow judges in a farmyard at eight-thirty in the morning. Most of the classes involved cattle, sheep and crops, so the yard was chockablock with Land Rovers and people in smart farming attire: jeans or moleskin trousers, brown work boots, and a checked shirt. There is rarely any deviation from this uniform. I had given great thought to what to wear today. Gardening clobber I thought would be a little disrespectful: gardeners don't tend to have a uniform for smart occasions like farmers do. Most of the gardeners I know are barely recognisable if you meet them in the evening – we scrub up well and often opt for fairly flamboyant clothing.

Today I chose dark blue jeans and a floaty shirt, coupled with shiny patent leather blue shoes that tie up with a blue bow, a rather large floral handbag and an extremely large costume jewellery ring. On reflection I did look a little like a dahlia amongst a row of potatoes (no disrespect intended to the farmers in attendance).

JUNE

I didn't know anyone in the crowd but they quickly picked me out as the gardener! As we all enjoyed coffee before setting off in our different directions, I subtly removed my bright green ring and slipped it into my handbag. I also quickly wiped off my lipstick. Gardening every day, you don't get the chance to smarten up often, but I must learn to tone down my garments when I do get let out.

A steward drove me around the country lanes to the seven private gardens that had entered the category. Sheer luxury to be driven and, as I admired the countryside from the passenger seat of the Range Rover, I felt a little like royalty. It's not to be underestimated how brave it is to open your garden for charity or take part in a competition. Gardens are such personal spaces. Those that do take the plunge should be encouraged but they must also be ready for comments that can cut like a knife or melt the heart. There's no accounting for taste, after all, and thank goodness we all desire different things from our gardens. If every plot were the same there would be little pleasure to take from visiting and we would be very short of conversation. Talking gardens is enjoyable and more importantly it's healthy – far better than gossiping about neighbours, other people's children or common ailments. Allowing people to poke around your perennials and peer into your pond is almost as personal as letting someone root through your wardrobe. "Oh, I don't like that top – far too sparkly!" "Those trousers are very out of fashion," and so on...

Visiting private gardens of all shapes and sizes over the years I have learnt that it's not just plants that are the focus. People are fascinating too. There's nothing better than being shown around a garden by its creator. Today I saw passion in bucketloads, and I experienced love. No, I didn't fall for a tall dark and handsome gardener! I witnessed people who were having a jolly good, life-enhancing romance with their gardens. The winners of the competition will remain a secret until the August show, but I can shout about how tasty the many slices of cake were that I was given on my judging journey. After all, what's a garden visit without cake?

CONSIDERING OPENING YOUR GARDEN FOR CHARITY? HERE ARE A FEW POINTERS:

- Never leave your smalls on the line.
- Put cushions on the benches and vases of flowers on the garden table for added flower power. Just choose your vase wisely: short and heavy-bottomed is best.
- Lock sheds that you would rather keep private (people are nosy).
- Put out photographs of what the garden was like before you started – this will impress everyone with the transformation.
- Never apologise – stand proud and stick by your decisions.

Thursday 21st June

My morning started with a jog through a field in wellies. No, this isn't a new faddy exercise regime! I've been moving sheep.

This week the lambs are being weaned from their mothers. Wearing wellies might not be as mad as it sounds on a warm June morning as the thistles in the sheep fields are at calf height. You'd quickly regret opting for unprotected legs. Gardeners and farmers are seldom seen in snazzy trainers and Lycra joggers – gardening is exercise enough for most of us and a gym membership is rarely relevant.

JUNE

The rest of the morning was spent in a far more sedate way, dead-heading roses. This is a pleasure. It's an opportunity to take in their heady perfume and admire the drama of the flowers. The roses in the garden here are on the whole unnamed; they were here long before me and names have mostly been forgotten. Amongst the ones I can identify are the creamy and highly scented 'Wollerton Old Hall' (named after the Shropshire garden I urge you to visit) and 'Tequila Sunrise', which I admire although it is on the gaudy side. Its bright yellow and orange blooms would be far more at home in a hot border than jostling with pastels in a cottage garden. A scented climbing rose with pale yellow petals that has lived here for years is called 'Schoolgirl'. A pretty but sickly rose is the stunning single pink 'Complicata' that falls prey to black spot. If single roses are your choice then the bright red 'Geranium' with impressive winter hips would suit a large plot, and *Rosa* x *odorata* 'Mutabilis' is a gem. It flowers nearly all through the year and offers pale pink, lemon and dark pink blooms. Being a species rose, it grows on its own roots, so you can prune it brutally to keep it to size.

The rest of the morning I spent pulling rosebay willowherb from the back of the borders. It's a big decision at this time of year whether to creep in and pull it – step into some beds and you risk knocking off the petals of foxgloves, lupins and poppies. Speaking of lupins, their first flowering is over, so I've cut back the heavy, faded flower stems. I'm hoping that there will be a second flush of flowers later in the year, although it's almost inevitable that the greenfly will get to them before I do. Delphiniums are stretching their arms up to reach above their neighbouring plants. I've resisted offering them any support as this is a sheltered spot. Joining them are the eryngiums with their thistle-like blue flowers. My favourite is most definitely *Eryngium alpinum*, one of the largest of the lot.

JUNE

I'm writing this entry with my computer perched on the potting bench. It's here that I wait for visitors to come and enjoy the garden. Today I can hear the chug of the baler as the hay is turned in the field over the road. A warning to those new to country life. The pressure is on for farmers, with haymaking and harvesting their only priorities. I marvel at the hours they spend at the wheel; after dark I can look out of my upstairs windows and see them combining late into the night. If ever I thought gardening was hard work, it's not a patch on being a farmer. Few of them have beautiful gardens at home, as they don't have the time to tend them, but if you think about it, they are gardeners on a much larger scale than any of us.

Monday 25th June

Gosh, it's hot. Far too hot to garden today, with temperatures reaching 27°C. I'm a typical English rose with pale skin: however hard I might try I crash and burn rather than tan.

The best way to deal with this weather is to get up early to garden, rest in the day (if life allows you to) and then head out again in the evening.

Today, my evening gardening consisted of weeding. As I worked in what still felt like blistering heat I was joined by all manner of flying insects. On hot days they are very active. However much I value the beneficial flying insects that pollinate our plants, today their buzz seems quite threatening. Strangely, I'm actually far happier with wasps and bees than flies. I suspect this harks back to my childhood. Grandmother's kitchen was often home to a good crop of flies in the summer, as the house was in close proximity to the farmyard that attracted them. I recall her telling my sisters and I about a vicar coming to stay, and that she had spent days clearing and chasing out flies before his visit. Every visible fly was banished. However, when the vicar sat down for breakfast and opened the box of cereal presented to him, a flying army was released. As a result, I am not a fan of fruit cakes – after all, who can tell the difference between a fly and a currant after being baked?

Retiring from weeding, I finished up by watering my pots. This evening the lily beetle was proudly displaying its red armour, although not for long, as it found itself between my fingers. You have to be ruthless or these dashing cavaliers will nibble both the leaves and flowers of the lily.

Tuesday 26th June

It's still too hot for any serious work.

In the garden the astrantia is striking today and the frothy lime green flowers of the *Alchemilla mollis* are at their very best. The first strawberries have ripened and in the hedgerows the sticky cleaver (*Galium aparine*) is certainly boisterous.

Wednesday 27th June

Today the temperature is still rising, as is the sting I got from a horsefly! Ouch.

Visitors to the garden have all sensibly arrived in hats. It's like Ascot here, with all manner of fashionable head-pieces on display. I left the house this morning with a straw hat more at home on a ranch than in an open garden. My son has specifically requested that I never wear it in public with him.

Today's tasks included dead-heading the peonies and a lot of watering of potted plants. My mother arrived with punnets this morning, fully intending to pick the blackcurrants in the fruit frame. I trotted along the garden with a cup of tea for her, but by the time I got there she had abandoned ship. Too hot.

When planting fruit bushes such as gooseberries, raspberries and blackcurrants in autumn, don't get carried away. The planting is the easy bit – it's the picking that takes dedication. Without my mother's eagerness to make jellies and jams I doubt I would get around to harvesting them all. The moral of this story is to grow only what you can manage to pick ... with one exception. Strawberries are never an issue – give a child free rein of the fruit frame and these juicy berries will certainly be eaten fresh from the plant.

Sometimes I fear that the new generation of children don't see fruit-picking as a fun pastime, as we did when we were young. I have very fond memories of my grandmother preparing fruits and vegetables that she had picked in the garden. She was always shelling beans, drying out walnuts to pickle and harvesting berries. Surely being amongst ripe berries and tasty fruits is a joy? The best bit, of course, is wiping your red-stained hands down your school uniform! (My thoughts on that, however, have changed now that I must do the laundry.)

Hemerocallis gall midge is an issue in the garden this year. This midge is seldom seen but the result of its work shows in distorted and very ugly flower buds, which need to be pulled off and discarded. Another pest that made itself known to me today is the blackfly. They have positioned themselves at the very top of the six-foot flower spikes of the *Inula racemosa*. After studying them for a while, and swearing at them under my breath, I watch the ants chasing them up the rear, keen to feast on the blackflies' honeydew.

Things to do

- *Put up shading in the greenhouse and open vents daily.*

- *Scatter some love around the garden by sprinkling love-in-the-mist (Nigella) seed in the borders.*

- *Keep on top of those weeds when you spot them – don't let them flower or you'll have plenty more.*

- *Sow some runner beans direct into the veg patch, and parsley seed into pots. (I've been taught to pour boiling water over parsley seed to help with germination.)*

- *Enjoy the peace and quiet of the plot. There will be footballs flying as you garden once the children break up from school.*

- *Buy some mini pumpkin plants so that you're all ready for Halloween (you'll thank yourself in October).*

JUNE

Country Project

DAZZLING CONTAINER DISPLAYS

Early June is the time to have fun with gardening in containers. In most parts of the country frost is no longer a threat so tender, half-hardy plants can be used to create wonderful displays.

I adore generous plantings of bedding plants and the thought of being able to reinvent the look every year appeals to me, so containers are a great way to make a temporary impact. I lust after a large copper planter – you know, the type you see planted with tulips at Sissinghurst Gardens. The ones with a price tag of about £600 plus? It's a fact that one large and impressive planter is far more of a design statement than lots of little pots all over the place.

Happily, however, there are less expensive ways to make an impact. Old tin cans, baskets, odd wellies and more can become part of your summer show. One of my favourite pastimes is to head to my local market town and rummage around for items that could be used as garden containers. Old apple boxes, tin baths and buckets are perfect for a country garden. I draw the line at old toilets, however – no one needs one of those in the garden!

How to create pots of colour

Anything can be used as a container, as long as it has a hole in for drainage in the bottom.

1. The bigger the group, the bigger the impact. Try to group your pots together this summer. I promise you that they will look far more impressive in one place.

2. First impressions count. Place all the plastic pots at the back of the group, raise them on bricks and put your attractive showpiece terracotta containers at the front.

3. Be slug savvy. Slugs and snails will enjoy the cool and dark cavern you've created by grouping containers. So keep an eye out and lift the pots to pick them off once in a while, before they settle in for a feast.

4. As for what to put in the pots – well, where shall I start? The world is your oyster. Personally I adore pots with height – a perfect combination being cannas and dahlias or for something more subtle and perfumed how about scented-leaved pelargoniums and creeping thyme?

5. Don't forget to water well rather than little and often.

Must-have plants

Acanthus spinosus
Alcea rosea
Astrantia major
Campanulas
(too many to mention)
Clematis 'Etoile Violette'
Clematis vitalba
Delphiniums
Echinops ritro 'Veitch's Blue'
Eryngium alpinum
Gillenia trifoliata
Lilium regale
Lonicera periclymenum
Lupins: Russell Group

JULY

I'm just grateful that they didn't head up my trouser leg!

Tool Kit

A good hoe (to keep on top of those annual weeds) and a Sussex trug or basket with handle (to look the part when dead-heading).

Two watering cans with long spouts that fit under your tap or water butt. One can fill whilst the other is being used.

Plant ties for climbers still in growth.

An old colander to keep in the kitchen garden to use when washing veg under the outside tap.

A spare cricket ball and a hard hat, a football and enthusiasm!

Cotton garden trousers – far comfier than jeans.

July

It might seem early, but July is the start of the harvest in the countryside. This month is a parcel of happy memories for me. School was out and I was free to roam.

The first of the winter barley will be cut at the end of the month so grain stores and machinery are being prepared. So many of my summer holidays were spent on the farm here. I recall my grandfather sitting way up high on the top of the combine harvester, looking down over the blades. No cab, no air con and absolutely no protection. As an adult the idea makes me scared, but as a child I was blissfully unaware of the risks. We simply had fun making giant nests in the cut straw and enjoying the family tea in the fields.

Our harvest tea always consisted of boiled eggs and fresh peaches picked from the garden. As a child I was a fussy eater, but these two country snacks were heaven-sent to me. I was the child who stole the peaches off the tree, although I denied it, of course! Nothing tastes better than a freshly picked peach – even the hairy skin isn't too bad.

JULY

Wednesday 4th July

We're in desperate need of rain. The clay soil is cracked and dry; it would be madness to try and turn the earth. Hoes are the only answer for keeping annual weeds under control in this heat, but the dust created by hoeing isn't pleasant.

It's frustrating to witness the prowess of the rosebay willowherb compared to the drooping of the lupins. With temperatures reaching 28°C day after day, it's tough to be a gardener at the moment, but not as tough as it is being a plant.

I'm a firm believer that watering should be reserved for plants in containers and those that water their lawns and borders should quickly rethink. Grass will turn yellow, but your lawn will recover. Plants in borders that are lightly watered will not put down deep roots in search of moisture, so in the long run you're killing them with kindness.

Visitors to the garden often ask me if perennials and shrubs can be grown in containers. The answer is that anything can grow in a container – even a monkey puzzle tree – but few will ever do as well as they would in the ground, and you'll have to commit to watering and feeding regularly. Containers are invaluable for creating a portable garden or adding interest to a paved area but as a gardener you must appreciate that they are putting the shackles on some plants, and that you're committing yourself to morning and evening watering throughout the summer. Much fun can be had planting pots but please remember that container plants need love and attention to put on a show.

Annuals are flourishing this week despite the heat. If your hanging baskets and container displays aren't looking good now,

JULY

then the chances are that they never will. Trailing lobelia, petunias and pelargoniums should be tumbling over the edge of window boxes and pots. To keep the displays going, dead-heading is vital. It's a light task that offers great rewards on a hot day. It's also a job that, with florists' scissors and a basket over your arm, can make you feel a little like the lady of the manor.

Dead-heading isn't just reserved for container displays, though. The borders need to be kept in check. Roses, hemerocallis, campanulas and lupins all need attention. Working in the borders I notice that the bright red berries of *Actaea rubra* are now with us. This plant has fairly insignificant white flowers in spring, but the berries sparkle for the rest of summer. They are poisonous but still earn their place in the garden. Towering over these low-growers is the lofty *Achillea grandiflora*. This generous, stately plant will certainly need support. Agapanthus are tight in bud and ready to explode into life – we grow many different types here, but I've got eyes on a new one, 'Twister'. It has white flowers with an inky base to each. Growing to about 55cm, this sun-lover will add height to a container display. They're perfect plants for pots as restricting their root growth encourages them to flower.

The climbers are the stars of the plot this month. Clematis never appear on a list of drought-resistant plants but I'm starting to think that, once established, some should be included. Honeysuckle is buzzing with bees, and this evening I spotted the first cluster of flowers on the campsis and the decumaria. *Schizophragma* and other wall shrubs are clothing the walls with glamorous foliage and flowers. Wall shrubs are not to be underestimated – they can help your home and garden hold hands, uniting them and working together.

I noticed today that the lettuce in the kitchen garden is flagging, but the tomatoes by the back door are starting to swell.

In this heat my legs are also starting to swell – another reason never to wear shorts! Summer is moving at a pace.

Thursday 5th July

The weather continues to be comparable to that of the Mediterranean. I'm in awe of how the plants are coping. If I stood out in the sun, fixed to the spot for a whole day, I would certainly curl up my toes.

My challenge today has been to try to identify a *Hemerocallis* (daylily). After an hour or so searching online, I almost gave up. I was recently reminded by a friend, who runs a nursery and is an expert on the daylily, that there are hundreds of registered daylilies, so it really is like looking for a needle in a haystack. I've settled on 'Stafford' but it could quite easily be 'Alan'.

The star of the garden for me today has to be the liatris, with its upright purple stems of flowers that are almost head height. The broad beans that were sown in November have been lifted and the rows that were planted in April are just about to produce their crop. Broad beans fresh from the pod are by far and away my favourite vegetable. Marrow comes a close second. I'll never understand why both of these vegetables are pushed to the side of many people's plates.

A walk through the cornfields this evening revealed a healthy crop of wild chamomile. This gorgeous little daisy with fine foliage is a native wildflower. It's a joy to see as a footpath walker but I'm sure the farmer would rather not have weeds in the crop. As I walk, I notice fat hen is robustly putting on growth in the cracked clay soil. I always find my summer evening walks insightful. Unlike walking through the garden, out here I'm happy to be met by weeds.

Friday 6th July

I'm writing this entry after finishing my gardening day with a little mowing at home. At 7.30pm the temperature was still generous, but needs must.

The grass is brown in places and now, where lawn daisies once thrived, I have clover flowers. The weeping willow has shed so many leaves it's a relief to collect them with the mower. I set to work in my bra and pants to tackle the lawn. Gardening in the countryside with no neighbours allows you to enjoy the garden scantily clad. I'm not one of those sensationalists who garden naked for media attention – I simply do it when it's too bloody hot!

Sunday 8th July

Today I have decided to embrace the heat and relax into it. I might want rain but the farmers who have started to combine certainly won't welcome grey clouds now.

My efforts to enjoy the weather have led me to be rather lavish: I've invested in a reclining chair for the garden. What a revelation! None of the other chairs in the garden are quite so comfy; they are designed as a place to perch for a quick rest. Having a chair that makes you put your head back is quite simply decadent. I lay for a good half an hour – a record for me –

looking at the blue sky, watching the dry leaves of the willow gently falling to the ground like feathers. This new recliner has made me realise the value of taking time out. After all, we garden to enjoy it, not just to be slaves to the plot.

By seven o'clock this evening I felt the heat had calmed enough to tackle the weeds in the path. I enjoy sitting on the ground and weeding cobbles and gravel, because the result is always so pleasing. My efforts this evening have been made all the more enjoyable by the discovery of a new tool. I've had a little hand-held hoe in my present box for a good couple of years, intending to give it to a friend. I decided to give it a go myself and what a pleasure it is. What a relief I didn't wrap it up and give it away.

Whilst sitting on the gravel I noticed that the cowslips that had been such a success in April and May were setting seed – I won't be weeding these out. Get down to ground level and you witness a whole other world of activity. I watched an army of ants marching past me and up the stem of a lupin. They seemed intent on reaching the top of the flower spike in search of honeydew – I'm just grateful that they didn't head up my trouser leg!

All in all, it's been a day to delight the senses. As I shuffled along the gravel path on my bottom, I enjoyed the scent of the mint I brushed past. It reminded me of the taste of the pea and mint dip I enjoyed with a French baguette at lunch: simply perfect for a hot summer's day. I can hear the slap of a cricket bat hitting a ball: my son is practising his batting skills in the field. I'm waiting for the call, "Mum – I can't find the ball!" Ball games are the best thing for a child but for a gardener they hold little benefit. At least a cricket ball causes less damage to my borders than a football.

Wednesday 11th July

Still no rain. The wheat has been harvested in some parts of the county and in the fields the cattle are lying still, save their constant chewing and swishing of their tails to flick off horseflies, trying to conserve their energy in this heat.

The grass on the lawn has stopped growing but the self-heal (*Prunella vulgaris*) is looking very well: the long gaps between mowing has allowed it to take hold. Another weed that is rising triumphantly from the dry soil in the garden and on the farm is the common ragwort (*Senecio jacobaea*). I am almost loath to mention this plant as it causes arguments every time its name is uttered. It's a great plant for attracting pollinators but many who keep cattle, sheep or horses are concerned it will poison their animals if it ends up being cut as part of a hay crop. Others are similarly convinced that it poses no risk to animals. I'm not a scientist, so I'm staying out of the argument, but I'm just warning you that if you mention this plant in your local rural pub, it's wise to set aside a few hours to debate it.

Sunday 15th July

We've had a gift – two inches of rain! This was the result of the most incredible summer storm. So sudden was the cloudburst that the drains quickly became blocked with fallen rose petals, and puddles formed all over the garden.

This morning revealed the results of such a downpour. Campanulas, eryngiums and hardy geraniums had fallen about the garden. The sheer weight of the rain caused chaos in the borders. Many flowers with metal supports had snapped where the support met the stem and could not be saved. To clear the paths for visitors, seven barrowloads of stems that had fallen over the path were cut back. It's a difficult decision to know how brutal to be when cutting back, but in an open garden you leave people to fight their way through the foliage at your peril. Few people want to leave with soaking wet legs.

The weight of the rain had caused the long stems of the kiwi to lower themselves to my height. Yes, we can actually grow edible kiwis in the UK if they are against a south-facing wall. To cut off the long stems, I reached up and snipped them with my secateurs, causing the water that was sitting on the leaves to rush down my arms. This got me to thinking about what the best things to wear in the summer garden are. In conditions like these, a light waterproof with elasticated wrists is a must. Usually I'm wedded to a loose-fitting smock top with three-quarter length arms. Long sleeves are a pain and very short sleeves leave you at risk from sunburn. I'm still struggling with the idea of wearing shorts in the summer (I think you've gathered by now that my legs aren't my best asset). I was wearing jeans when the rains fell. Disastrous choice! If jeans get very wet they quickly become incredibly heavy and a few inches longer, and end up dragging on the ground in the mud. Wearing wet trousers brings back bad memories of having to swim in pyjamas for a school lifesaving badge. (I failed!)

I was thrilled to spot that the wisteria has produced a second set of flowers. These are smaller than their forerunners but still a joy to have. Joining this climber is another highflyer: the campsis is in full flower now and adding interest to a south-facing wall. The giant tree lilies at the back of the borders managed to stay upright in the rain. Their buds are still tightly closed but their eventual pink shade is now evident. Crocosmias are offering incredible colour; the red of 'Lucifer' is my favourite. These plants are so difficult to identify. I also grow Crocosmia 'Emily McKenzie' and it's almost impossible to spot the difference between these two.

In the fruit frame, a feast of raspberries, loganberries and gooseberries are on offer. As today is the men's Wimbledon final, I see this as a fitting time to pull up the strawberries, which have been disappointing this year, and start again. Strawberries are short-lived plants, so for continued, guaranteed success they need lifting and replacing every three to five years.

I am beginning to question the value of petunias as bedding displays. Out of all the plants in the garden they look the most bedraggled after heavy rain. Their flowers hang like wet tissues on the plants. *Calibrachoa* 'Million Bells Series' (often referred to as mini petunia) are, on the other hand, amazing at putting up with anything the weather throws at them. I'm naturally drawn to white flowering plants, but perhaps my allegiance to them is also fading. White flowers look exceptional in evening light, and they offer purity and freshness, but as they fade and go over they look much messier than any other colour. I suppose it's to be expected – we all know how tricky it is to keep that pure white linen shirt sparkling after a few washes.

Thursday 19th July

A burning July question: Weed or wildflower? A weed is simply a plant in the wrong place. Every morning I'm completely appalled to meet a dandelion in the garden, but equally thrilled to admire it in the hedgerow on my evening country walk.

At Stockton Bury, there's often a sharp intake of breath when a visitor to the garden spots a weed. Their face is a picture of disgust – it's a similar look to a friend spotting dirty dishes at the sink. Consider your friends' kitchens. I expect that, like me, you'll have some who have clear surfaces and shiny kettles; others that don't even have space to rest a mug on the counter; and all sorts of people whose kitchens are somewhere in between. We all keep our homes in different ways, so it confuses me that gardeners think a plot must be kept completely weed-free.

A garden should reflect our personalities, lifestyles, location and time restraints. It is therefore completely acceptable to have weeds if you want them.

Personally, I'm happy to keep a few in the garden. I'm more than happy to have *Clematis vitalba* (Old Man's Beard) clambering over a garden hedge. Red campion (*Silene dioica*), common dog violet (*Viola riviniana*) and tufted vetch (*Vicia cracca*) are all welcome. Nettles are even allowed in places, under a warning – one step out of line and I'm in there with my fork. They're adored by pollinators, after all, and they can be used to make a rather stinky, but very handy, organic plant feed. My philosophy is to treat weeds like the family pooch – allow them free reign until they get over-excited. You must remain in control at all costs or they'll run away with you. (Mark my words: I am a terrier owner who knows how hard it is to be the master!)

Wednesday 25th July

The school holidays have started and so, contrary to popular belief, garden visitor numbers drop off. Grandparents are on standby for babysitting duties, gardening clubs are on hiatus with members on holiday and families have flown to warmer climes.

JULY

Mind you, this year I'm not sure you'll find much warmer than here. Although we experienced heavy rain a few days ago here, in many parts of the country rain is still something gardeners are dreaming of – are we ever happy with what the forecast brings?

The garden at Stockton Bury is holding up surprisingly well in the heat. Lilies are spectacular this week, their scents heightened by the warmth. Their perfume is so evocative it transports me to more tropical places as I pass by with my wheelbarrow. Another smell that evokes instant memories is that of the fig tree on the dairy wall. Planted over 150 years ago, the smell of it reminds me of my childhood: for me, its foliage is the scent of summer.

Verbascums and *Eurybia* x *herveyi* offer vibrant yellow and purple in the borders. Another rather dashing partnership is *Clematis* 'Jackmanii' and the golden hop. Lime green and purple is always a combination that works well. Agapanthus and dahlias are also adding a flamboyant touch to the garden.

Speaking of flamboyance, in the spring a row of gladioli corms were planted in the veg patch and they're now in flower. These are for my mother, who is banned from wielding her secateurs elsewhere in the garden. She is welcome to cut these for church flowers but nothing else. When you look after an open garden, the last thing you want is an over-enthusiastic florist in the family. Cutting flowers is a sin here – even if you're a regular churchgoer. My recent discovery when it comes to cut flowers is that a bunch with a few stems of mint added goes some way to keeping flies out of the kitchen. Flying doodle bugs that seem to land on anything you fancy eating are in fine fettle. The heat obviously suits them. Flies are my least favourite of God's creatures.

Saturday 28th July

Gardening has been a dusty affair this week. This morning I decided to cut the aquilegia right down to the ground: the foliage was spoilt with mildew. My hope is that fresh leaves will form before the summer is over.

Whilst rummaging on hands and knees in the borders to cut back this cottage garden favourite, I was showered with seed. I'm half expecting to have a real granny's bonnet by next summer! As I worked through the borders, I spotted a rather stunning dierama (angel's fishing rod) with perfect pale pink bells. This is the most elegant perennial in the garden. They're not easy to keep: a wet and cold winter can be the death of them. I leave their foliage in place over winter to offer some protection but that's still no guarantee, so I'm delighted to see this one in bloom.

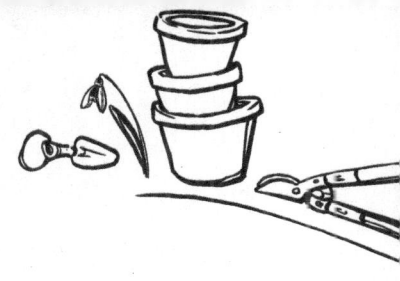

Things to do

- *Water first or last thing in the day. When the bats start flying in the evening, I know it's time for my daily watering.*

- *Plants in terracotta pots tend to dry out quicker than those in plastic, so water well.*

- *In very dry weather cut back on mowing.*

- *Pick your courgettes whilst they're young, and pod your broad beans in the garden. Preparing veg outside is far more fun.*

- *Keep the garden looking smart by dead-heading and staying on top of annual weeds.*

- *Cut faded lupins right back – you never know, they might flower again.*

- *Go to RHS Hampton Court: wear a hat and take plenty of bags for plants.*

Country Project

SUMMER GARDEN PARTIES

If you live in a rural setting, eating out means just that! Make the most of the light evenings by sharing the garden with friends.

I'm not house proud, so if friends are coming for a meal in the winter you'll find me racing around with a vacuum. It's for this very reason that I prefer to socialise in the garden in summer. My lawn is usually in a better state than my carpets. Even in the garden I'm guilty of looking at what needs doing rather than relaxing. To prevent this, I keep a table and chairs in a paddock – that way I can look at the view beyond and forget about the to-do list. The downside is that the paddock is rather a walk from the house, so setting up for a meal involves at least half a dozen trips back and forth, but it's worth it.

Instead of rolling sausages around on a barbecue and trying to keep a conversation going through plumes of smoke I'm more of a garden salad and cold meat kind of girl. And as far as I'm concerned, the only pudding that should be allowed at a country garden party is a bowl of home-grown soft fruit.

In the centre of my garden table is always a large and heavy vase of flowers and foliage. That, and a large glass jug filled with cool water and ice cubes with a borage flower at the centre of each. Of course, the children will shun this for something less healthy and the adults will turn to the wine! I have a large collection of much-loved family china that is past its best so guests are given chipped and odd plates outdoors, but somehow this adds to the party mood. As well as it being the environmentally friendly option, if you aren't up to clearing the table at the end of the evening, china plates won't blow away!

JULY

Top tips for summer party success

1. If you don't have a big enough outdoor table, recycle some old wooden pallets. Place a row of them two high on the grass and cover with a tablecloth. Your guests can lounge on blankets and cushions on the floor.

2. Instead of a vase of flowers, why not put a pot of scented thyme on the table? Add some citronella candles to keep the insects at bay and you will have a sweetly scented table to dine at.

3. Whatever you're feasting on, I find that before pudding a garden game goes down well. Egg and spoon or sack race can be great fun for all ages, or set a treasure hunt for children.

4. Old jam jars decorated with glass paint can be used as tea light holders that can be hung from tree branches, or fill a glass salad bowl with water and float flowers on the surface of the water with floating night light candles as the light fades.

5. A fire pit is a good focal point for the evening, and you can add a whistling kettle for hot drinks on tap. Provide plenty of blankets to go over knees, and enjoy the perfect setting to watch bats swooping and diving.

Must-have plants

Anemone x hybrida 'Elegans'
Cyclamen hederifolium
Echinacea purpurea
Eucomis comosa 'Sparkling Burgundy'
Eupatorium maculatum
Hosta plantaginea 'Aphrodite'
Roscoea purpurea 'Red Gurkha'
Rudbeckia triloba 'Prairie Glow'
Sanguisorba 'Blackthorn'

AUGUST

Giggling from within
the borders

Tool Kit

Empty ice-cream tubs, which will be useful when picking soft fruit.

An old-fashioned scythe.

Brown envelopes for saving seed, and an old biscuit tin or plastic storage box. Save silica gel sachets to add to the seed store (hunt in your new handbag or anything you purchase for the little sachets!).

Seed for sowing now: winter-flowering pansies, pak choi, spinach 'Perpetual'.

A homemade frame of chicken wire and an old wheelbarrow to dry onions.

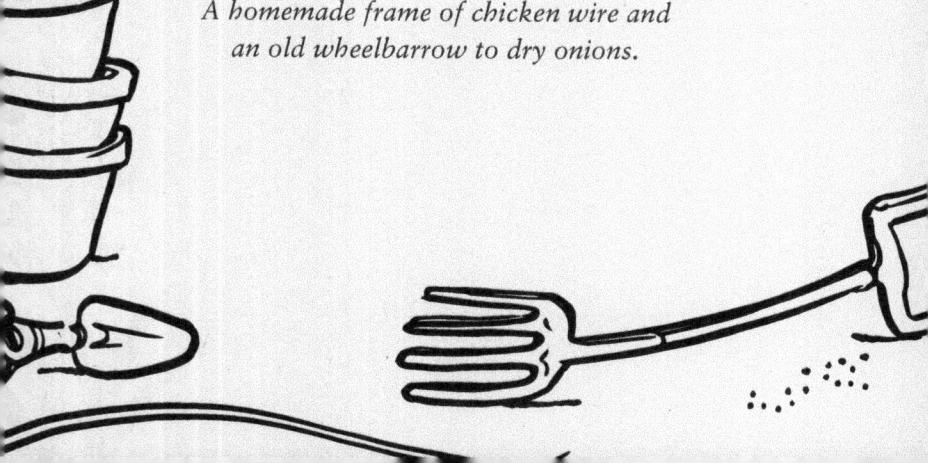

August

Gardening in August can be tricky. It's often too hot to tackle heavy jobs (or even light ones) and it's very difficult to know whether to cut back or hold up some of your plants. It's a time to edit, dead-head and drink lots of water.

That's not to say that there isn't colour in the borders – celebrate hot colours, dramatic shapes and interesting textures. It's one big, often unruly, party in the garden.

On the farm, combining is in full swing and straw is being baled. With the long days come baskets of boiled eggs, flasks of tea and sandwiches being ferried to the fields. By the end of the month, farmers don't want to see another sandwich as they have had them for breakfast, dinner and tea.

As you drive along country lanes you are likely to see the odd farmer kicking the wheel of his tractor. Breakdowns at this time of year seem all too frequent (machinery breakdowns, I mean, although if it rains a lot there could be some farmers on the edge themselves!).

Thursday 2nd August

Silly season has arrived – the entire world is on holiday and it's therefore impossible to arrange anything with anyone.

Even garden clubs are taking a break along with the Prime Minister and the groups that were set to visit us this month dwindle in number by the day as their organisers receive call after call with people dropping out.

The attitude towards the garden from our visitors also changes dramatically this month. I am always shocked by the number of people who expect an open garden to be just as perky in late summer as it was in May. Gardeners are capable of a lot, but they cannot keep a garden in 'May and June attire' all summer long. It takes nerves of steel to open in August, as you can only hope that visitors understand that this month is associated with slightly unruly plants. In amongst them, though, are gems that sparkle and giggle from within the borders. Campsis, clerodendron, lilies, althaea, eucomis and roscoea are all exceptional right now. Why oh why don't we all embrace the month we are in, throw our arms open wide and love what it has to offer?

Combine harvesters are still offering the backing track to gardening and the hedgerows are displaying a feast of ripening fruits. I grew up on damsons as a child – served with cream in a delicate, white china bowl.

The countryside is a picture with fields littered with golden straw bales – the fields are certainly in order, whereas the garden, by comparison, is rather less organised. I feel it's only right to add a warning to those hoping to buy a home with a small bit of land in

AUGUST

the way of a paddock in the country. Managing a field or paddock is not to be underestimated. If you have a couple of acres, it will be too tricky to mow – fields need grazing or cutting for hay. It's certainly not viable to buy your own tractor and cutter, so you must put yourself in the hands of the local farmer. I can tell you for sure that your couple of acres is not a priority to them at this time of year, even if you are offering to pay. Getting the harvest in is all-consuming and they probably haven't even had time to eat at the table this month. It's quite likely that you'll end up with a paddock shoulder-high in docks, nettles and grass if you don't plan ahead for the management of your plot. You might want to consider a few sheep!

Today in the garden I continue to look for rosebay willowherb in the border, in order to pull it before it sets seed. It's become a daily challenge to see how far I can lean into the border to eliminate this cunning weed. Even more of a priority than pulling willowherb was to search the garden for debris. Last night, Stockton Bury was used as a location for a photoshoot of locally crafted fire-pits. The challenge was to shoot six fire-pits throughout the garden: different models, with different things cooking on them, photographed in different settings. In a few hours we mocked up Bonfire Night, Father's Day, breakfast and evening drinks. I'm not often in the garden here in the late evening, so witnessing the warmth of the light from the fire was a pleasure. Stockton Bury feels a completely different place as the light fades, and I love it. It's the only time of day that I feel inclined to sit down and not work.

The evenings are drawing in already, and last night the light faded quickly. By 8.40pm we were running out of time. The shoot concluded at 10.00pm and we were left looking for wine glasses, blankets and marshmallow prongs with only the light of our mobile phones. This was good enough for us to spot a giant toad, however, who is obviously king of the garden at night. I'm sure he was very annoyed to have our company.

After my search for abandoned props was complete, this morning I pulled up some annual poppies that were long faded and looking very burnt by the sun. I also decided to cut back a boisterous perennial sweet pea. This pea had taken over an area of about 4m^2 – I was surprised to find that, even after weeks of dry weather, the soil was very damp under its cushion of foliage and stems.

Revelation of the day – *Phlox paniculata* 'Mount Fuji' smells like the curry plant. I'm not sure I like it.

Thursday 9th August

This morning it was so peaceful in the garden. I spent a few happy hours in the water garden, clearing the leaves of faded plants that were overshadowing the streams. With this very hot summer continuing, I'm keen for our visitors to enjoy the cooling trickle of water in The Dingle.

In this part of the garden, the pickerel weed (*Pontederia cordata*) is still a show. It has been displaying its blue spikes of flowers for weeks and weeks. Around the edge of the pond, keeping its feet dry, is the lofty eupatorium. These plants are just about to flower and, alongside anemones and echinacea, offer the perfect August display.

The garden is loaded with ripe seed pods: if they all explode at the same time we'll be showered in seed and might even sustain a light injury. Just a few minutes of working in a border leaves me

AUGUST

with a head full of poppy seeds. Border work is essential at this time of year – especially if you open to the public. Each day I am selecting my next culprit to be cut back. If a plant offends the eye, and I'm not planning on saving the seed, it gets the chop. The trick is to cut perennials right back to the ground. You might not get a second flush of flowers, but all being well you should get some low-growing fresh, more compact foliage. If you grow alstroemerias, which I have great success with here, pull the stems out of the new hybrids after flowering. Pulling rather than cutting encourages them to grow more vigorously. As for hemerocallis, which I have been dead-heading daily, I have recently discovered that if you leave the flowering stems to turn brown you can simply pull them out of the plant. This is so much quicker and more satisfying than cutting them out leaving a stump.

In the kitchen garden, the heat has resulted in some exceptional peaches and a bumper crop of figs. Sinking my teeth into a juicy peach always reminds me of my childhood. I would steal them off the trees here at Stockton Bury, hoping no one would notice. Of course, everyone knew I was the guilty party because I would enter the house with a juice stain down my top! Today, the tomatoes that are growing outside the back door are also rather tempting – they are grown in terracotta pots rather than gro-bags and accompanied by clay pans of French marigolds. The marigolds are said to attract the whitefly, keeping them off the tomatoes. Whether this works no one really knows, but they do look rather good together.

I've noticed today that the dahlias that were left in the garden to overwinter have flowered. I adore dahlias but my uncle has fallen out of love with them. I can see how this would happen; lifting tubers in autumn can be quite a task, especially if you garden on heavy clay. If lifted, our tubers are stored on a plastic sheet in the cellar, which remains at a constant 6°C. My grandmother always used to grow rows of dahlias in the kitchen garden. They were a carnival of colour. I'm keen to grow more just because they remind me of her. It's so wonderful when you associate a plant with a certain person. I wonder which plant will make my son think of me? I'd be happy with almost anything but a tough old parsnip.

I was reminded earlier today that I garden in the heart of a farm. The hose pipe that I use to top up the rill doesn't have a snazzy tap attachment – instead it is held to the tap with a milking teat secured with black gaffer tape. Waste not, want not!

Friday 10th August

Today we've had a little rain – not enough to stop me working in the herb garden, though.

I've been pulling faded foxgloves and sprinkling their seed at the back of the border, and lightly trimming any herbs that, after a hot few weeks, have lost their zest for life. The borage and calendula were beyond help, however, and have been completely removed.

Herb gardens always have a sell-by date. Lavender, rosemary and sage become woody and leggy after a while and anyway, I think it's good to re-evaluate your cooking habits every five years – do you still cook a lot with thyme or sage? If not, replace them with something else. Plan your herb garden around your own culinary habits rather than being tempted by a random selection of interesting plants – herbs are there to be used and if they remain unclipped they will suffer.

The topic of the day in the border between myself and Colette was poisonous plants. As we delved in to cut back *Aconitum* (monkshood), we reflected on the story of a gardener who had sadly died after working around this plant. Many, many moons ago, aconitum was ground down into a powder and arrows were dipped into it and then fired at the enemy to poison them. There are so many poisonous plants in our gardens – lily of the valley (*Convallaria majalis*) is a shocker – but if we rid our gardens of them all it would be a disaster. Their beauty would be missed and, let's face it, we all love a plant that comes with a little drama. The secret is to learn which plants are a danger and work responsibly with them.

Speaking of history, my first visitor to the garden today spotted a copy of *The RHS Plant Finder* on the shelf above my potting desk and remarked on it. He explained that he was a dentist, and one of his patients was Chris Philip, the man who came up with the initial idea of *The Plant Finder* and edited the very first edition in 1987. According to my garden visitor, Chris was looking for a particular plant and thought how wonderful it would be to be able to find all the nurseries in one book. I use this book daily, so I am thrilled with this story. The retired dentist went on to explain that Chris was a genius at creating firework displays on a huge scale – it's little facts like this that make my day and reaffirm that gardening can be just as much about people as it is about plants.

Later that day, I mentioned the story to my uncle. "Oh, yes, Chris – he came here often!" My uncle went on to share stories of Chris Philip's visits here, which encouraged me to Google his obituary. What an incredible man. The firework displays that his dentist casually mentioned were in fact the displays put on in 1977 for Her Majesty The Queen's Silver Jubilee outside Buckingham Palace!

In fact, it isn't unusual for my uncle to announce in passing that he knows or has known someone exceptional in the horticultural world. As a teenager, I recall the famous plantsman Christopher Lloyd coming here to visit. If only I had known I was in the presence of such a great man! All I remember is that he commented on how much he liked my rather bright purple jumper, which makes good sense when you consider his bold use of colour in the planting at his garden, Great Dixter in East Sussex. I have kept that jumper to this very day.

The final task of the day was to head up the ladder to deadhead the lilac. Some might say that this is unnecessary, as they drop their petals so quickly all by themselves, but its faded flowers are offending my eye. As we are on the subject of history, it was always thought to be terribly bad luck to cut lilac flowers to bring them into the house. The maid who picked them would have been in trouble for bringing a plant inside that shed its petals all over the place. I wouldn't mind a few petals strewn around my house. However, I am pretty fed up with the mulberry tree dropping its juicy fruits on the lawn. I have known gardeners to cordon off mulberry trees to prevent visitors getting their clothes stained. The juice is almost impossible to remove from fabric and from fingers – you have been warned.

Thursday 16th August

After a few decent showers of rain the garden is looking wonderful. There is so much going on here with plums, kiwis, apples, figs and mulberries ripening fast. It's like being in the garden of Eden with temptations all around. I haven't yet spotted a naked Adam in the shrubbery, but I keep looking.

AUGUST

Visitors are surprised how green the garden is after such a dry summer. They are even more surprised when I tell them that we don't own a hosepipe (apart from the very short one I use to top up the rill). Leave plants to go thirsty and they will put good roots down in search of a drink (apart from those in containers, of course).

Today I have been moving faded plants out of the 'show' greenhouse and adding in some more treasures that have been hiding in the 'backstage' polytunnel. The chrysanthemums have been flowering their socks off since May under glass and now have no colour, so they have been replaced with a rather dramatic *Amorphophallus rivieri* (devil's tongue). This tender but easy-to-grow plant is rather sinister in appearance, with a thick stem that has markings like a snake. To add to its charm, when in flower it stinks of rotting meat, which attracts the pollinating flies. The deep maroon goblet-shaped flowers are fantastically phallic. How dramatic and how exciting.

I've been thrilled to see that some of the campanulas that were cut back by half only a few weeks ago have reflowered – albeit not with the same vigour, but flowering all the same. The aquilegia has also bounced back with a fresh head of foliage after being cut to the ground.

This is definitely a week for dahlias and I regret not planting more of them in early summer. These blousy flowers had fallen out of favour up until a few years ago but they are now very much admired. Their resurgence in popularity I put down to Sarah Raven – her inventive use of them in planting schemes and her skills with colour are to be congratulated. My own dahlia-based top tip is that if your dahlia flowers and foliage are being nibbled, and you can't see any sign of a pest, the culprit will probably be the nocturnal earwig. To trap them, place an upturned plant pot stuffed with straw on the end of a cane and the earwigs will hide here in the day. They can then be squished if you're up to it.

Thursday 23rd August

The madness of this summer month continues and, as usual, the weather for the bank holiday weekend is looking wet.

We have been blessed with good rain at night and the garden has bounced back in a remarkable fashion. It is for this reason that I am frustrated by prospective visitors who call to ask if it is worth coming! Imagine asking a gardener if their garden is worth a look? It's like asking a chef if their meal is worth eating.

White and pink Japanese anemones are spreading joy around the garden and the asters (I refuse to use their new unpronounceable name *Symphyotrichum*) are sprinkling magic through the borders. Today I have been looking for the white tips of the autumn crocus (*Colchicum*). They need to be revealed in the borders or they'll be missed. All the perennials that overlap them are cut back to allow them to sparkle. Elsewhere in the garden, *Cyclamen hederifolium* is out; it seems early, but I am reliably informed by my Twitter family that they are out in Northumberland and in the south. It seems strange to see them when we still have the odd wisteria flower. The agapanthus have been incredible this year, but I think next week will see the end of their display. I am constantly being asked by visitors why their agapanthus might not be in flower. These plants need sun, plenty of water, a fairly tight-fitting pot and – this is the secret – repotting into fresh compost with a slow-release feed added. So few gardeners give their container-grown plants

AUGUST

new compost or feed in March or April. You can't expect them to thrive on fresh air alone.

As expected, the lawn that was like a door mat a few weeks ago has bounced back and greened up. It's quite remarkable how resilient grass is. It proves that August is a growing time; I look around the garden and see plenty of new growth – especially from the climbers. A remarkable find for me this summer has been the *Hosta plantaginea* 'Aphrodite'. It has very plain green leaves that you could easily ignore, but the flowers that appeared just last week are packed full of scent. All the other hosta flowers here have faded so this is an unexpected treat for August. Visitors seem very smitten with the *Hydrangea aspera* Villosa Group with its purple, flat heads of flowers, and those with a good eye for detail have spotted the *Lobelia laxiflora* with its yellow and orange blooms.

For sheer flamboyance, the gladioli in the kitchen garden are keeping me well stocked with cut flowers now that the sweet peas are fading fast. I wish I had planted more zinnias and cosmos but I haven't got room. Even in a four-acre garden it's possible to be short of space – you simply can't have it all. The petunias in my container displays, however, are looking a little like wet socks after the heavy rain. It's the pelargoniums that I rate for coping with all weathers. Sun or rain they keep on going.

I'm writing today's entry at my kitchen worktop. My walk with Larry has been cut short due to a downpour. As I look out of the window it appears the trees have started to do a salsa – even their trunks are swaying in this strong wind and rain. The danger of heavy storms like this is that the weight of the leaves and the stress of a very dry summer can lead to large branches falling. For this reason, you won't catch me pitching a tent under a tree in August!

Whilst skipping home from my walk through the rain showers I spotted hedges laden with ripe fruit. The elderberries are ready, as are the blackberries. Plums are sheer perfection, but the damsons and apples are not quite ripe for picking. Patience is not a virtue I possess. I tried to eat a 'Laxton's Superb' apple today, but abandoned the attempt: I fear a whole one might lead to a tummy upset. I am slightly put off from eating unripe fruit by an experience I had as a child. With about twenty acres of cider apple trees on the family farm, October half-term holidays were spent picking them up from the ground and putting them into sacks. My sisters and I would relieve the boredom by daring each other to eat the small cider apples. Being the most competitive, I fear I overdid it and suffered an Enid Blyton-style stomach ache that I will always remember. Lesson learnt.

Saturday 25th August

Disaster – I popped to town today to buy school uniform with my son as it was too wet to do much else. I quickly realised that I had been walking around the shops in a mud-splattered jacket and pair of trousers I'd obviously been kneeling outside in.

The moral of this story is to have one wardrobe for the garden and one for going out in public and never the twain shall meet.

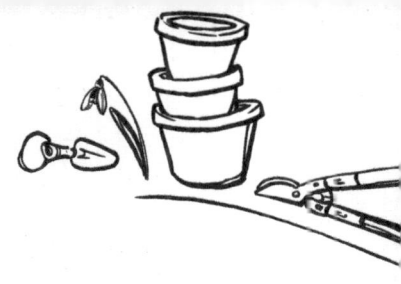

Things to do

- *Ignore your lawn but cut your wildflower meadow. (Forget the brush cutter, use a scythe and enjoy hearing the birds as you work.)*

- *Put house plants outside, especially if light rain is forecast.*

- *Plan the last evening garden party early in the month, before the evenings get shorter.*

- *Edit your borders, cut back perennials that have faded (unless you want to save the seed) and prune wisteria and lavender.*

- *If eating plums straight from the tree check the fruit for wasps before you take a bite.*

- *Visit open gardens and embrace the month of August.*

- *Camp in the garden. There's nothing like unzipping the tent early in the morning and being met by a glorious summer garden.*

AUGUST

Country Project

STORING HOMEGROWN ONIONS

Love or loathe onions they are undeniably one of the most useful vegetables, whatever your style of cooking.

I'm no onion expert but I adore seeing them drying out in the August sunshine. My uncle has an ingenious way of drying them. He has made a wooden frame with a chicken wire inner and it sits over the top of an old wheelbarrow. The onions are placed on the chicken wire and the barrow is used to move the onions into the sun. It's then easy to rush them under cover when rain threatens.

Onions are easy to grow from baby onions (sets) and this is far quicker and easier than growing from seed. Our sets are planted in April and will be ready to harvest this month. The small sets are planted in rows about 8cm apart and pushed into the well-turned soil so that their tips are just showing. The south-facing vegetable garden here is perfect and the pH of the soil is about 6.5, which is ideal for onions (they're not keen on an acid soil).

You'll know when your onions are ready to harvest as the foliage starts to turn yellow and flop. After lifting they need to be dried for up to two weeks. Once dry we plait them and hang them under a veranda. These long strings of onions have an incredible appeal simply as a decoration. An old brick wall decorated with onion plaits is a sight to behold.

How to make an onion plait

Plaiting isn't easy but it's certainly worth a try. A well-plaited string of onions is the perfect gift for a friend.

1. Start by cutting a piece of string (about 15cm long).
2. Tidy up your onions by removing any loose outer paper.
3. Trim off the bits of root.
4. Choose three onions to start.
5. Place the three onions on a work bench (outside, as it's messy) and start to plait.
6. Add another onion to the top of the plait and fold that into the plait. Keep adding the onions as you add a section. Keep untangling the ends as you go.
7. When your plait is long enough (I would suggest about 12-15 onions) stop.
8. After the last onion is in place finish plaiting the foliage and tie off the end with the string and hang up. Chop the end of the plait off for a tidy finish. It is now easy to cut individual onions off without the plait falling apart.

Must-have plants

Agapanthus 'Peter Pan'
Anemone japonica
(my favourite is 'Pamina')
Apios americana
Dahlias (in all their
dazzling outfits)
Eucomis pole-evansii
Eurybia x herveyi
Humulus lupulus 'Aureus'
Hydrangea aspera Villosa Group
Kniphofia rooperi
Miscanthus sinensis 'Malepartus'
Rudbeckia laciniata 'Herbstsonne'
Sanguisorba

SEPTEMBER

The familiar smells of autumn return

Tool Kit

A very large jam pan, lots of empty jars
and plenty of sugar!

Sharp secateurs. Don't wait to put them
on your Christmas list – you need them now.

Garlic corms to plant.

Bulb catalogues. Don't miss out on those
tempting spring-flowering bulbs, and plant
hyacincth bulbs now if you want flowers
for Christmas.

Cold frames are a very handy addition
to a country garden.

New thermals – it's getting colder.

September

The garden closes to visitors at the end of this month. Although I shall miss the company, it's time to think of new ideas to tempt gardeners back next year. Planning and planting will consume hours of my time but we must be realistic about what we can achieve. Any new project that's started now must be completed before the gates open again next April.

This is also a busy month on the farm. The rams that have spent the year on their own in a secluded paddock are released at intervals into the girls' accommodation.

It's best to avoid too many lambs arriving at any one time – as with vegetables a glut is tricky to manage – so the rams are restricted to a few groups at a time. Now that harvesting is finished, autumn cultivation begins straight away, and hedge-trimming is the task when the soil is too wet to work.

At the end of the month you'll be able to munch your way around the countryside – blackberries, sloes and wild strawberries will keep you well fed.

Prepare yourself for a glut of produce by eating up the boring things in your freezer to make way for more tasty country and home-grown goodies.

SEPTEMBER

Thursday 6th September

The children are back at school and some semblance of order has been restored. I can now garden without a twelve-year-old on my heels asking me how long I'm going to be! The washing line will no longer be decorated with holiday swimming trunks and beach towels but instead it will be sporting a row of white school shirts.

With the start of a new school term come the familiar smells of autumn ... including the whiff of muck from the cattle yards being spread in the surrounding fields. As I walk through the garden, the occasional thud of an apple can be heard as it drops: it won't be long before the season of mists and mellow fruitfulness is upon us. The autumn crocus (colchicums) are in full flower and look spectacular. If you thought that interest in the garden was fading with the light, you'd be very wrong. There's plenty in flower with waterlilies, *Eucomis pole-evansii*, sanguisorbas, *Eurybia* x *herveyi*, *Apios americana* and dahlias putting on a rather wonderful Indian summer display.

Today has been spent harvesting seed. Armed with lined cardboard boxes, I leapt into the borders with my secateurs. I cut back the stems of the biennial *Smyrnium perfoliatum* – one of my favourite plants for interest in the spring – and the sea holly (*Eryngium*) and placed the cuttings in the boxes. There's no point trying to strip the stems of seed in situ, as you'll lose too many in the border, so you're far better taking the cuttings to the potting shed (or, in my case, the dairy) in a box, paper bag or old pillowcase and sorting them there.

Our dairy looks like a laboratory at this time of year: clear plastic bags filled with seed pods hang from the ceiling, jam jars are stuffed with berries and cardboard boxes littered with seed. For the best results, seed should be collected on a dry day. In some cases, it should be sown straight away – I'm a great believer in following what nature does. If the seed is dropping to the ground in the garden in early autumn and producing a crop of new plants in spring, why go to the bother of labelling and storing it? Just crack on and sow it and save yourself the bother.

In the vegetable patch, I've harvested a barrowload of marrows and squashes and there are plenty of carrots ripe for pulling. Despite all this vegetable-themed excitement, my mood was quickly flattened by the sight of the gooseberry bushes. They've been completely stripped of foliage by the gooseberry sawfly. The result will be a weakened plant and less of a crop next year. It reminds me to check the roses, which can also be attacked by sawfly at this time of year. Speaking of loss, the euphorbia that I cut back in spring hasn't come good so I've dug it out – never mind, room for a new plant.

There are still some autumn raspberries to be picked, which may be required as a snack when next weeding – that is, if the blue tits don't get to them first. On arrival at the fruit frame this morning, I witnessed a miracle. One moment, two tits were in the frame and the next they were the other side of the net. How they got through so quickly I will never know. The frame is covered in chicken wire, but I now know it has holes too large to keep out small birds. I've finally removed the padlock on the gate of the fruit frame this week: after all, there is little left now for garden visitors to munch on if they venture inside. It might seem greedy to lock a fruit frame, but I wanted to ensure that the August cherries were mine – all mine!

Elsewhere in the garden, it appears that the roses have had a third wind. Nearly every rose has at least one new fresh bloom today. 'Gertrude Jekyll' is offering a flutter of reliable pink flowers and 'Wollerton Old Hall' is displaying a delicate cream bloom. It's almost as if they are having their last hurrah before summer is over. The rather gaudy yellow and orange 'Tequila Sunrise' is still flowering, just as it has been all summer.

I'm not a fan of its colouring but it behaves as if it's running off Duracell batteries. Why is it that the rose you are the least fond of keeps flowering? I suppose it's a way of sticking two fingers up at the disapproving gardener.

I'm writing this at 8.30pm and it's pitch dark outside. One of the benefits of the darker evenings is that the chickens go to bed early. In the summer you have to stay up for hours before they head for home. Something to think about, if you're considering keeping poultry.

Wednesday 12th September

Driving home late from giving a garden club talk tonight, I was struck by the verges glistening with dew.

The blades of grass looked as if they had been individually brushed with silver. This evening's talk was in the idyllic setting of Bibury in the Cotswolds; being a village of such beauty and stature there wasn't just one but *two* pictures of the Queen in the village hall!

Thursday 13th September

It's amazing how quickly the seasons change. In just a week, autumn has arrived. A week is a long time in a garden.

The foliage of the *Cercidiphyllum japonicum* tree is releasing a candyfloss scent from its leaves and is the first to show the fiery

SEPTEMBER

colours of the season. I have this tree to thank for the change in attitude of our visitors towards the garden this month. As soon as autumn colour is evident, people are happy to be presented with seed pods and at last stop expecting to see roses, lupins and geraniums. With the impressive TV coverage of show gardens, I fear that garden visitors expect to be met by perfection. A garden like this one, though, moves with the season and has a soul that twists and turns in a different way with each passing day.

In the last few weeks we have been lifting overcrowded clumps of bulbs to sell or replant in the borders. I've harvested the bulbs but have yet to replant them. So, for now, they are in a bucket hanging on a hook in the garage, in the hope that the mice won't be brave enough to creep up that far to steal them. Those clever little chaps are amazing acrobats and seem to be able to scale almost any height in search of a meal.

Mice, voles and shrews are regular guests in a country garden. If they sit still for long enough, you might have a chance of detecting which is which. Mice tend to have large eyes and ears. They are often the guilty party when it comes to nibbling your kneeler or munching on your broad bean seeds. Voles have smaller eyes and ears, a shorter tail than a mouse and are very shy. It's quite unusual to see voles during the day. Shrews also have a fairly short tail in comparison to mice but are easy to spot thanks to their pointed snout. It's the shrew that will nibble the buds of your clematis if the plant is left to trail across the ground. However, the shrew will also eat slugs, so you might want to welcome them. I don't mind sharing the garden with a few of these tiny mammals but a RAT – I'm afraid I'm completely terrified of them.

Plants that I adore this week are the climber *Apios americana*, the coleus in the greenhouse, the passionflowers and the roscoea *Eucomis* (pineapple flowers) are still flowering, but as they are so heavy they have flopped under the weight of their large blooms. We still have a few sweet peas hanging on for grim death, and the fuchsias, although still flowering, are flicking their dead-heads around the greenhouse floor with wild abandonment. Shocking pink cosmos are flowering their socks off and I'm keenly dead-heading them to keep the displays going for as long as possible.

Top tip: keep your eye out for seedlings in paths and borders. This week I have created 30 new plants – *Campanula lactiflora*, *Carex buchananii* and eryngiums have all been lifted and potted on. They'll be perfect for planting out next spring.

Tuesday 18th September

This month is flying past faster than any other. Today, the high winds that set deciduous leaves into flight have given us all that autumnal feel.

The car and garden, and even rooms in the house, are covered with the seeds of silver birch now that the catkins are breaking up. There is natural litter everywhere. Every paved surface in the garden is covered in the seed of the silver birch, which means there will be plenty of little seedlings to pull out next year. My mood has changed from feeling frustrated about summer passing to embracing autumn. I'm not sorry that the garden looks more of a free spirit than a perfect vision. I compare it to a school child who hasn't brushed their hair, has their shirt pulled out, socks down and scuffed shoes but still somehow has a certain charm. Nothing is trussed up now – the garden is showing its true personality.

The lawns have been cut today and, in the process, a few windfall apples have been sliced in two by the mower blades. The thud as they fall to the ground is almost as good a sound as a six being hit on the cricket field.

I've also been dealing with the arrival of a large bulb order from Holland. The dairy is full of alliums, amaryllis, narcissus and crocus bulbs and eremurus (foxtail lilies). The spidery form of the eremurus root is simply exquisite: it looks like it belongs in a glass cabinet in the Natural History Museum.

Bulbs are so exciting to be around because there is so much promise and energy stored in them. A few years ago, I noticed some allium bulbs very close to the surface of the soil. I assumed that heavy rain had washed off some of the top soil. On closer inspection, and after a little careful digging with a trowel, I realised that the bulbs were being pushed up and out of the earth by their friends and family below. I lifted a clump the size of a breeze block, carefully pulled them apart and replanted them in the garden. What I've learnt from this is to get up close and personal with your plants. Nine times out of ten they will tell you when they're in trouble.

A mystery has been solved this week – we were convinced that we had a rather stinky blocked drain. I now discover that the apios (groundnut) that climbs around the door of the visitor's toilets has a strong smell. Never has it had so many flowers and never before has it been so pungent. I can only describe it as the smell of a stable yard – old leather and horse manure! A fascinating climber but not one to plant too close to the house.

Friday 21st September

Blackberry-picking continues in the countryside and the farmers are out hedge-cutting. We have 22 miles of hedges to cut here on the farm.

My uncle was remarking today how he has cut these hedges for over half a century. Again, evidence that gardening is just farming on a very small scale. Thankfully I have never yet been let loose with a tractor and trimmer. I'll stick to my hand shears and a stepladder.

The last time I mentioned garden pests I was lamenting the rodents and picking on the gooseberry and rose sawfly. This time I am enraged by a mole. In a private garden, it is possible to put up with the odd mole hill, but in a garden open to the paying public they do not go down well. You're stuck between a rock and a hard place. Visitors aren't happy to see an invaded lawn but, equally, don't want to see mole traps. I have heard of gardeners putting their radio by the hole to scare them off (moles don't like noise) and recently someone recommended to me that a man should wee by the mole hill. I'm happy for a garden to be used for most things, but widdling and piddling I am not!

Tuesday 25th September

I've been sorting through the recent delivery of alliums, narcissus and tulips.

We're having our first bulb sales event this weekend, but I hope there will still be plenty left to plant here in the garden. I've got my eyes on the bulbs of *Allium* 'Pink Jewel', and for height and splendour the giant *Allium* 'Ambassador'.

I know you'll find this hard to believe if you have a smaller plot, but we really struggle to find places to plant bulbs in the four acres at Stockton Bury. My uncles have been planting for 40 years and there's layer upon layer of plants here. Most bulbs require a well-drained and sunny spot along with 90 per cent of other garden plants – and there are only so many perfect locations to go around.

As I sorted the bulbs into fives and tens to sell, I was reminded of childhood visits to the Post Office for sweets – the scrunching of a paper bag is a sound I could listen to all day. In the early 1980s you could buy a packet of Polo Mints for 4p. You can't even buy the paper bag for that today.

Thursday 27th September

Today was by far and away the most beautiful day we've had this year. The sky was clear blue. The garden was packed with vivid colours, both from leaves turning golden and outrageous flowers belonging to the likes of the kniphofias and nerines. I'm in heaven.

It's on days like this that you are paid back for struggling in the cold and wet of winter. I'm thankful that my life path has led me to working outside. I spent the morning cutting a huge bucket of flowers – with only a few days left of the open season, at last I can freely harvest bunches from the garden. Two vases of dahlias, rudbeckias, eupatorium, alstroemeria and anemones are now proudly displayed on the potting bench.

My new secateurs have been put into action this morning and veratrums that have flopped to the ground, crocosmias and campanulas have been cut right back. I've promised myself that I'll wipe the blades of my new secateurs off with an oily cloth at the end of every day to keep them clean and sharp. Secretly, I know I'm fooling myself – I'll never be that organised.

Friday 28th September

Autumn is all about being in the right place at the right time. Today the show of autumn leaves was at a peak, and against a clear blue sky it was simply wonderful.

There's still much to be done, though, so I couldn't stop to linger too long. With only two days left to go until we close the garden for the year, it seemed the perfect day to start clearing the veg patch.

The soil is warm, dry and easy to work. The skeletal sweet pea plants clinging to their hazel supports for dear life are easy to pull from the ground. Before lifting them, I searched the row for seed. You're looking for seed pods that are paper-bag brown with seeds that are solid and black. When you flick the seed out of the pods, it should be so hard that it almost bounces back out of the bag at the speed of an air-gun pellet. Thanks to the dry summer, my sweet pea seed harvest was pretty dreadful, so I'll be buying some fresh this year as well.

Behind the sweet peas stands a row of gladioli that is more foliage than flowers. Once the leaves have gone yellow these will need lifting too, and the corms dividing. As I clear the marrows, squash and sweet peas, I'm already thinking about what to plant next year. I'd still love a row of dahlias here. But discussing this addition with my uncle didn't go well. "I can't start giving up my veg patch for cut flowers," he replies. And that's that. I'm not going to win this argument as he never shops for vegetables and is completely self-sufficient all year round. Who am I to get in the way of such an annual achievement?

The hop string that is woven neatly between the arms of a scaffold frame for the runner beans has also been cut today and the exhausted beans dug up. Some see this annual ritual as a sad time, the end of an era, but I love seeing bare, freshly turned soil. Having had a very traditional route into horticulture, working with my uncles and in a parks department, I'm all for neatly clipped edges and bare soil. That's not to say that I don't appreciate gardens that are glorious in their wild abandon. I just wouldn't want to be gardening there.

The distinct smell of stable yard outside the visitor's toilets has now gone as the flowers of the apios have shrivelled. Elsewhere in the garden, the eucomis have started to flop, unable to hold the weight of their huge flower stems any longer. The foliage of *Viburnum opulus* is scorching red and nearly all the leaves have fallen from the cercidiphyllum. The Asian pears (*Pyrus pyrifolia*) are ripe and ready – you need to time it just right, as windfalls aren't very good from this tree; they seem to rot as soon as they hit the ground. I notice that all the fruit on the lower branches has already gone. Perhaps Adam and Eve have dared each other to steal a pear rather than the more traditional apple as they wandered the garden. Heaven knows there are enough apples in Herefordshire! I don't fear that they will go to the devil – instead I expect they tasted a little bit of heaven when they sank their teeth into such a juicy fruit. I'm just annoyed that I missed the visit from Adam again!

Along the top path, the towering stems of *Inula racemosa* look ready to be cut to the ground. As I move the cut stem from the plant to the barrow, they release the most incredible cloud of seed. So much seed, in fact, that you could recreate the scene from the 1970s film of *The Railway Children* when Roberta sees her father appear from the steam on the platform (for me, the most emotional movie scene ever).

Saturday 29th September

One day to go before the gates of the garden close for another year. I'm always slightly relieved not to be answering gardening questions every day and constantly checking that the toilet roll hasn't run out, but I will miss the company and the characters who come and share the garden with us for the summer.

A couple who visit regularly told me that they had given each other a hug under our monkey puzzle tree for the last time this year, but will return to hug under it again next year. How lovely. It's not unusual for people to come for one last visit in this week to "have our final quick fix before the winter." This is a phrase I hear time and time again (along with, "Have a good Christmas!"). How lucky I am that I have the arms of this garden wrapped around me the whole year through.

When I look back over the summer, the garden has played its part in making memories for so many people. We've had brides and grooms visit to have their wedding photos taken, people celebrating birthdays and anniversaries, artists and photographers and even one young man who sat in the garden and quietly played his guitar.

On a more sombre note, we have also had visitors who have come for their last visit ever. It is not unusual for the terminally ill to choose a garden visit as a way to spend time with their friends. I hope that those who joined them here will forever hold this garden in their heart. We hope that when we open again next spring, our regular and much-loved customers will be able to come once more, having had a healthy winter. So many people feel safe and loved here, where they are able to laugh, reflect and relax.

Gardens are more about people than plants and their importance to us should never be underestimated.

Things to do

- There's still time to sow salad leaves direct – September tends to offer great growing weather.

- If you plan to open your garden for charity next year, register your interest this month.

- Buy bulbs – lots of one type rather than a few of each. Less is more, if it's impact you're after.

- Visit a garden full to the brim with dahlias and make note of the ones you want to grow next year.

- Attend a seed swap.

- Put the contents of past-their-best summer container bedding displays on the compost heap and clean the pots out.

- Cut asparagus foliage to the ground once it has gone yellow, and order asparagus and rhubarb crowns now.

- Sample apples in friends' gardens before choosing a new tree to plant next month.

SEPTEMBER

Country Project

SAVING AND STORING SEED

This topic comes with a warning. Collecting seed can become an addiction.

If you're anything like me, you'll have drawers, pockets and envelopes stuffed with seed you're never likely to sow. If I were to sow all the seed I collected each year I'd have seed trays covering every square inch of my home and garden. I do always look out for local seed swap events (although, again, if you're anything like me, you'll return with more than you took with you!).

The good news is that seed kept dry will last well – even beyond its official use-by date. You might not get the expected rate of germination, but it's worth knowing that some seed can germinate decades after being created. Seeds represent hope. However old and wise you get, the joy of watching something that looks as if it belongs in a funky new brand of herbal tea transform into something, in some cases, large enough to stand under, never gets less exciting.

But remember, not all seed needs to be stored. Some, such as foxgloves, poppies and one of my favourite biennials, *Smyrnium perfoliatum*, can be harvested and scattered immediately where you want new plants to grow. Mimic nature, drop the seed when the plant would, and you won't go too far wrong. It's sowing seed that gets most of us into gardening in the first place. The desire to babysit actual children might fade with age but the desire to grow from seed only increases.

How to collect, store and sow seed

1. Assess your plants. In most cases, seed is ready for collection when seed pods are dried out and paper-bag brown.

2. Choose a dry, calm day. You want your seed to be moisture-free. Avoid high winds, for obvious reasons!

3. Use old pillowcases when harvesting. Put your stems in whole and sort the seed indoors.

4. Remove any plant debris and leave the seed spread out to dry inside in a lined, open cardboard box. Make a note at this point of what's what! Once dry, you're ready to put the seed in envelopes.

5. Store dried seed in a paper envelope (so you can write on the outside the name of what's inside) and place inside a sealed plastic box in the fridge, or an airtight biscuit tin with sachets of silica gel to absorb moisture.

6. Before sowing your seed, you'll need to research the requirements of each individual plant to find out how and when you'll have the best chance of success. Whatever you're sowing, use the right compost. A seed compost will offer far better results than a bag of multipurpose.

SEASONAL TREATS

June

Sadly the asparagus has come and gone, but there's plenty of salad leaves to be had and radish are growing at a pace. The autumn-sown broad beans are ready – if I could only grow one vegetable, it would be broad beans. Their flowers are edible but don't be tempted to eat too many or you won't get any beans. The flowers taste like – you guessed it – broad beans and add a little glamour to a mixed salad. For pudding, what can beat a bowl of freshly picked strawberries? Mind you, it's rare that our strawberries make it into a bowl. I'm guilty of pinching them as a quick on-the-go snack when gardening. If you haven't grown strawberries in your garden, head to a pick-your-own place with the kids – they'll love it.

July

The fruit frame is fit to burst with blackcurrants, summer raspberries, loganberries, nectarines, peaches and cherries all ripening. Get those freezer bags ready so you can store gluts of fruit or plan a garden party and offer your guests a fruity selection of desserts – it's the perfect time to put summer pudding on the menu. The garden offers lots of opportunity to decorate your edible offerings. Sprinkle calendula or borage petals on cakes and salads to wow your guests. A few petals can add a little charm to a cake that hasn't risen! Don't forget to pick courgettes when young – they taste fantastic. You won't know what to do with too many giant courgettes later in the summer.

August

Plums are juicy and ripe, so perfect the art of making pastry and put plum pies on the menu. If all else fails keep a few rolls of the ready-made type in the freezer – no one will ever know. Cucumbers and tomatoes might be ready for picking. I adore the yellow cherry tomato 'Sungold'. Its small golden-yellow fruits are a perfect, sweet snack to break up the monotony of weeding. Maincrop potatoes are ready to harvest – ours will be stored in the cellar in a nest of straw. If you've got plenty of carrots, then now's the time to hunt down a recipe for carrot cake. Don't look to me for a cake recipe, however. I was never destined to be a baker.

September

There's no excuse not to eat seasonally this month, with beetroot, runner beans, French beans, potatoes, carrots and the last of the salad leaves on offer. Tomatoes are ready to pick, as are the figs. If the weather suits, you'll also be picking the autumn raspberries, blackberries and the first of the apples. It's the month to have a feast. You could almost lock the house up, put up a tent and survive by foraging entirely from the garden. Just think – no washing-up for a month! If you do decide to stay put and not decamp, it's also the time to perfect the art of making chutney and jam. Put an order in for Kilner jars and get busy – homemade preserves make the perfect Christmas gift. Could it be time to join the Women's Institute?

Must-have plants

Acers
Asters (Symphyotrichum)
Colchicum autumnale 'Album'
Cosmos bipinnatus
Dahlias
Euonymus alatus
Hydrangea paniculata
Ipomoea tricolor 'Heavenly Blue'
Malus x robusta 'Red Sentinel'
Nerine bowdenii 'Zeal Giant'
Rudbeckia fulgida
Stipa gigantea

OCTOBER

No coming back from
death by choking

Tool Kit

A bulb planter or transplanting spade.

A metal dustbin with heavy lid to store chicken feed in (rat-proof).

String for your conkers.

Old pallets to make a leaf mould box.

First aid kit for the shed.

Apple peeler – you'll be making apple sauce and apple crumble nearly every day.

Freezer bags for freezing damsons.

Sharp pruning saw and secateurs.

A battery-powered leaf blower.

Horticultural fleece to protect plants from sharp frosts.

October

On country roads you've been stuck behind farmers hedge-trimming last month and now it's time to sit behind tractors pulling loaded trailers of cider apples and potatoes. Before you curse the inconvenience, consider how much you enjoy a local cider! Please don't race around impatiently – didn't you want to escape the rat race?

My advice is never to try to overtake – just pull into a layby and look at the view for a while. After all, if it wasn't for the farmers there wouldn't be such a view, and if they didn't cut the hedges you'd hardly be able to drive down country lanes, let alone overtake.

Planting is the main task for farmers this month. They plough the field and scatter the good seed on the land then they hope that it is fed and watered by God's almighty hand. The sea gulls are visiting Herefordshire, although we are about two hours from the coast. They have come for a seed feast. It's very strange to hear a sea gull in these parts.

In the garden leaves, leaves and more leaves fall but there are still a few reminders of summer with some roses still blooming Tree and bulb planting time is upon us and my thick winter tights are yet again pulled out of the drawer!

Monday 1st October

Yesterday I stood under a horse chestnut tree, watching my son play football. During the game, I collected a few shiny conkers to give to the children. As I filled my handbag, I wondered why I was the first to collect them in such a public place.

When I presented the team with a fistful of polished conkers, the response from one of the boys was, "What are these and what do we do with them?"

This comment has left me concerned for the future of our countryside. I'm convinced that half the population are walking around with blinkers on. Yes, a vicious game of conkers might be a health and safety issue for schools but more of an issue is the complete lack of interest in our trees. Surely it's not too much to ask for children to know a handful of native trees before they leave primary school? I clearly remember going on nature walks with my class. On my dressing table I still have a small stick I collected when I was about eight years old. I asked my uncle to mount it on a block of wood and for the last 40 years it's been where I hang my necklaces.

Before I forget, I have one word to say to you all today – RATS! This is a warning to all those living in rural areas. The rodents are coming in from the fields, looking for dry winter homes. You have been warned.

Wednesday 3rd October

What a day! I've just spent the morning at Raymond Blanc's Belmond Le Manoir aux Quat' Saisons on a gardening course with Jane, the talented chef of our garden cafe.

I'm familiar with this garden after writing about it many times for magazines so it was great to be back, especially at this time of year. The beds were full of pumpkins, colourful rainbow chard and beans packed with ripening seed ready to be collected for next year's crop. For lunch, we were presented with shredded celeriac and mustard, and warm crusty bread made with potato and beer alongside a hot parsnip soup. This gardener's feast was eaten in the heart of a stunning glasshouse surrounded by pots of chillies, displays of marrows and baskets of crab apples. It certainly felt like the perfect way to mark harvest. Parish churches will be celebrating harvest festival this weekend and, although some may not like my comparison, today I felt that this greenhouse packed with ripening and vibrant fruits and vegetables was my church.

Leaving the garden, we met Raymond's head gardener, Anne Marie Owens. She was clutching armfuls of ripe eating apples that she'd just polished, ready to deliver to the hotel. To lighten her awkward load, she gave us both an apple for the journey home. For some reason an apple from Raymond's garden has a sweeter taste than any other I've tried. Today has given us plenty of ideas for our café menu next year and new varieties to sow for the garden, but, more importantly, we have embraced the month of October and fallen in love with it all over again.

Friday 5th October

Now that the garden gate has been shut for another year at Stockton Bury it's all go. If one more person says, "You can put your feet up now, Tamsin," I will jump up and down with those very feet like a spoilt child.

We have more to do in this month than any other. It's in October that we sculpt the success of next year's garden. With four acres to put to bed, and very few hands to help, I've already started work in the borders. The hollow stems of the giant *Allium* 'Ambassador', with their huge dead flowerheads at the top that remind me of a Japanese straw hat, are so exhausted by their summer efforts they can be simply pulled out of the ground with two fingers. Bearded irises need close inspection before you cut to ensure that you don't damage the newly forming leaves that lurk behind the old, and you must also be careful not to step on the tiny cyclamen as you work.

The roses are still blooming but the temperature is good (12°C). *Rosa* 'Tequila Sunrise' is not giving in (I'm sure it knows I'm not keen on it!) and *Rosa* 'Peace' has the most wonderfully scented pale lemon blooms on show. Joining them in the borders are the bright orange *Kniphofia rooperi* (I counted 32 flowers on our cluster of plants) and the pale pink flowering nerines. These are two perennials that I won't be cutting back just yet. When the kniphofia are over I'll dead-head them and then take a third of the foliage off by putting it in a ponytail and trimming it.

As I cut back faded campanulas under the witch hazel, I spot the tiny brown flower buds of its scented winter flowers. Tucked right up against the trunk of this plant is a neat cluster of *Cyclamen hederifolium*. I love the way that these miniature plants pick little hidden places to grow – it's almost as if they are trying to hide, or forcing us all to get on hands and knees to admire them as they just peep out from under deciduous shrubs. I suspect that if plants had a sense of humour, these cyclamen would be the cheekiest.

The bucket of a tractor is our barrow today – this saves hours of walking backward and forward to the compost heap. The other essential of today's work is the cake that waits in the porch for us all at teatime. With the garden café closed, we simply must munch our way through the array of leftover lavender shortbread, beetroot brownies and carrot cake. A good gardener seldom needs to worry about their weight and my diet will be mainly cake and tea this month. A hungry gardener is no use to man nor beast.

We've also been dismantling summer bedding displays. The geraniums have been cut back by half and potted up to spend the winter in the heated polytunnel. This polytunnel has the thermostat set to just above 2°C. This winter retreat isn't always a success as geraniums often succumb to mildew but it's worth a go They've been flowering for weeks so they deserve a little bit of attention now – the most important thing is to resist watering them too much.

Monday 8th October

The weather is dry and sunny and the ground is friable. Perfect weather for planting more bulbs.

Following our bulb event, we have a few that failed to sell and are left for us to plant. They have been stored in a cool, dry and darkish room but the *Fritillaria persica* and *Fritillaria* 'Ivory Bells' have started to form small roots. They are obviously desperate to find soil. We have twelve of each to plant; at a cost of around £10 a bulb we can't afford to get the placement wrong. Bulbs of such value need a premium well-drained soil and a sunny spot.

As I've mentioned before, finding a space like that is nearly impossible here. After a lot of head-scratching, my uncle wiggled his way through the border to find gaps and, using a narrow transplanting spade, began to dig. It looked like a giant mole had been very hard at work. Each bulb was then carefully placed in the hole and back-filled. It goes without saying that to plant bulbs of such a size is almost impossible if you haven't cut back the borders yet. A top tip for cutting back borders is to leave stumps on the lilies and other bulbous plants so that you don't accidentally slice through them with a spade.

There is nothing more exciting than bulb planting. If you're moving to a new house in the not-too-distant future but can't resist the allure of bulbs, plant them in aquatic baskets and sink these into the border. These can then be lifted and taken to your next garden. Although planting bulbs is one of autumn's highlights, if I'm given the choice a visit to an arboretum today would have been the only thing to top it. Autumn is at its most beautiful now. One minute the *Parthenocissus* is a sight for sore eyes and the next it's over. Blink and you'll miss the best of the season.

Monday 15th October

The rain is falling, and autumn has quickly gone from being rather dramatic and breathtaking to being horribly miserable.

Thankfully the polytunnel is watertight and has a radio. This is where I hide on days like this. I'm in the mood to organise the plants today and get rid of those that have failed or outstayed their welcome. I'm ashamed to admit that a few agaves have made it into the "don't want" pile. They might be stunning, but they are lethal. You could easily lose an eye if you fell into one of these spiky succulents and when you are open to the public, things like this need to be considered.

It's a great time of year to have an autumn clean undercover. You need to clear room in your greenhouse so that tender plants can be brought in before the frost arrives. All our evergreen agapanthus are in, lined up and ready to spend winter listening to Radio 4 with me. I am not as organised as I should be and have plenty of plants without labels. Some pots look as if there is no sign of life at all within the soil. However, before you fling them, empty them out and investigate – you might be surprised at what you find. It goes without saying that all plastic pots should be saved and used again. We have hundreds here! Store them out of the sun and they'll last longer.

The cider apple harvest continues in earnest. Most lunchtimes I walk through the orchard to my mother's house – she makes great soup! Negotiating a field littered with small apples is like trying to walk through town on roller skates.

Wednesday 17th October

Last night I gave a talk at our local village hall. Everyone in the audience has probably known me since I was a child, which is a rather strange scenario. Each of them will report back to my mother about my performance, so the pressure was on.

The village hall in question is a traditional 'hut' that hasn't been polished, buffed and rebooted – it's exactly as it always was, which adds to the charm. It took two of us to pull the bolt to open the door and upon entry it was freezing cold. However, after about half an hour of intense heat from overhead electric bar heaters it was like being a piece of toast under one of those old-fashioned gas grills. This was the hall in which I learnt to Scottish country dance as a child and it's also been the venue for many local funeral wakes. It holds memories both good and bad but, as with all old village halls, it's a vital part of our community and I secretly rather love it.

The evening started with a member of the group announcing that she had found a kitten in the road and it needed a home. Impressively, it took only about three seconds for someone to throw their hand up. After that rather charming start, I was on. No point giving much of an introduction here. RHS judge, ex-editor of a well-known gardening magazine – none of it is relevant. I'm just Tammy, the skinny girl who used to ride around the village on a podgy pony as a child, displaying a rather impressive set of buck teeth.

I'd arrived with a bucket of Asian pears (*Pyrus pyrifolia*) and one of the group had kindly washed and sliced them to share amongst the audience. As I described the wonders of the Asian pear tree the plate of sliced fruit floated around the audience with the elegance of the ambassador's silver platter of Ferrero Rocher and eventually ended up back with me with one slice left – how polite. I was feeling rather chuffed with the success of my food-tasting idea. Until ... someone started to cough.

Emergency dash through the thick red curtain that divided the hall from the kitchen to grab a glass of water. Panic went through me as I filled the glass. There would be no coming back from death by choking at one of my garden talks, and in my village to boot! I was doomed. What would my mother say?

After a few heart-stopping moments the lady in question recovered – phew! I think I might reconsider the food-tasting segment in future; my nerves can't take it.

The start of my day was much less dramatic. I've had a peaceful time in the secret garden, cutting back perennials and planting

Allium cristophii and *Allium* 'Firmament' bulbs. Larry, my Border terrier, has been tethered to the gate – leave him loose and he'll be off chasing rabbits and I don't have the energy to hunt him down. If you plan to garden alongside your pooch, take my advice and don't choose a terrier: take a leaf out of Monty Don or the Blue Peter Team's book and go for an eager-to-please Labrador.

My barrow today has been the front bucket of a tractor again. I really must master driving a tractor, rather than relying on my uncle to empty the bucket. Can I do it? Not so sure. Leave it with me.

After using my handsaw to remove a branch from a *Magnolia* 'Butterflies' tree (wonderful yellow flowers), I could start the bulb planting. My handsaw is definitely on its way out. The handle is broken and held together with red tape. As I cut through the branch I smiled to myself – how many years have I written in various publications about using a good, sharp saw? Perhaps I should make a side note to say that even a sharp blade is no use if your handle falls apart!

After a day of gardening, by three o'clock I found myself sitting on cold stone slabs that edge the border, digging holes for my bulbs. Yes, I know that sitting on cold stone is said to lead to haemorrhoids, but I'll deal with that if it happens. A day of crouching and bending takes its toll and when you need to sit you need to sit. It would be sensible to park my bottom on a kneeler but mine has been nibbled by mice in the shed and then chewed enthusiastically by the terrier.

Friday 19th October

Ouch! I've cut my finger with the secateurs. Having managed to avoid a secateurs injury for years, it was overdue. This is when gardening on your own becomes tricky.

OCTOBER

You have to make it from the garden to the house and then into the First Aid box without dripping blood all over the show. I'm very squeamish about the sight of blood so I put my muddy finger in my mouth and left it there until I reached the sink. The problem with gardening hands is that they are so ingrained with mud it's almost impossible to clean a wound. A plaster, a chocolate brownie and a cup of tea later and I'm ready to go and empty my wheelbarrow.

Joking aside, if you have a large garden it's worth keeping a First Aid box in the shed at the other end of the garden. It never hurts to be prepared. Why not do a First Aid course? It's wise to be able to treat yourself, if nothing else.

Up until the finger-meets-secateurs incident, the day had been going very well. Today was a typical autumn day and the first time that my fingers felt the chill. My fleece headband was given its first airing of the year. I find these so much better than woollen hats. A headband doesn't get as itchy and if you have ears that stick out like mine there is always the hope that they might remain pinned back once you remove it. Worth a try!

The dahlias are looking spectacular today – so much so that I picked a bunch for my mother. Dahlias are very generous plants that you shouldn't be put off growing just because they might need lifting in winter. Another plant that took my eye today was *Lysimachia clethroides*. This hardy perennial, which I admit can be a little invasive, has wonderful autumn foliage. Its white summer flowers are bee and butterfly magnets in summer.

As I work my way through the borders, I have my eyes peeled for clematis. There are many planted in the borders here in amongst the shrubs, and if I accidentally cut them off at the base there will be no flowers for the following year on some varieties. There are three different pruning groups for clematis. Group one (which mainly includes early-flowering clematis such as montanas), do not require pruning. Those in group two (large flowering hybrids) need light pruning in February and flower on the previous season's growth and group three flower on new growth and need pruning harder in early spring. Don't panic, though, as specialist growers will give details on the label, but if you do have an unknown clematis in the garden then try to identify it before you get busy with the secateurs.

Wednesday 24th October

A glorious day! There were five of us in the garden today, working away, and two of them were in shorts. When I worked in an office, days like this would make me question my desk job. Everyone should want to be outside gardening in this weather.

Clear blue skies and autumn leaves are a fantastic combination. Ironically, I spent the day preparing for frost. The fuchsias that have spent the summer in the greenhouse in the kitchen garden have been put in a barrow and wheeled to the cellar. Lifting a large standard fuchsia in a terracotta pot is like lifting a three-tier wedding cake into the back of a car. It's tricky. Once they reach the cellar, they're placed by the door, so that they have light and a frost-free home for winter. Some of these fuchsias have made this journey for over 20 years. The greenhouse is now completely empty apart from a couple of passion flowers that have rooted in the beds. What incredible flowers these are.

In the borders, it's the monk's hood (*Aconitum*) that has the first prize for colour. Shocking blue flowers couldn't fail to impress, but please remember that they are highly poisonous – they're the devil in disguise. The asters and nerines still sparkle and under this sky the colours are electric.

Apples are plentiful here, but the Asian pears are over. A basket of home-grown kiwis met me as I went to the house. Very tempting, but sadly as hard as bullets. The summer hasn't been long and hot enough to ripen them even though they have been grown against our south-facing wall. In two months' time, after they've had time to soften, these will be turned into the most delicious conserve. The large 'Brown Turkey' fig by the house is quickly losing its leaves; you can see the tiny figs that will provide next year's feast. This wonderful fig is the second oldest plant in the garden after the monkey puzzle tree. Once the leaves fall, its gorgeous tracery of silver stems will be revealed – for me this is when the fig looks at its most resplendent.

I took my coffee break by the pond near the beehives. Gosh, the bees were active today – enough to make me a little nervous about being stung!

Thursday 25th October

Bulb planting was on the agenda again today. Colette and I faced the challenge of planting a couple of hundred narcissi bulbs in a root-packed ground under some mature shrubs.

We started with small hand trowels, but as the challenge progressed the tools got larger and larger. The most effective was, once again, a trusty transplanting spade. As we tried hard to dig, Larry watched with a smirk. That dog is a master at digging holes just where I don't want them! Today he was not for helping. Bulbs should be planted at two and a half times their depth in a clay soil but, between you and me, some of these daffodils might be a little closer to the surface than that!

After the shrubbery, planting continued with giant *Fritillaria imperialis* bulbs in groups in the Pillar Garden. These impressive spring-flowering plants will add a Mediterranean feel to the borders next year, but to put on a show they need plenty of sunshine. Their large bulbs have a hole in the middle, so my uncle always places the bulb at a slight angle and then covers the top with a leaf from the tulip tree (*Liriodendron tulipifera*) before the soil is replaced in the hole to cover the bulb up. His thinking is that the leaf will prevent the hole in the bulb filling with soil and reduce the chance of the bulbs rotting. Whether this is effective, or just an added distraction, I don't know, but it felt like I was undertaking a ceremonial burial.

The autumn leaves of the tulip tree are covering the main lawn, so to be honest I was glad to bury even a few of them with the bulbs. This giant rivals the neighbouring monkey puzzle tree. No, it isn't related to the spring-flowering tulip – its summer flowers are of a similar shape to a tulip. You need a large garden to accommodate a tree of this size as it can reach a hundred feet. Our specimen was planted in 1977 to celebrate the Queen's Silver Jubilee. There were two specimens at the tree nursery when my uncle went to buy it. One tree came to us and the other was planted at Hereford Cathedral by HRH The Queen (my uncle swears he chose the best one!). I was four when it was planted and it was probably five years old itself when it went into the ground here. It's rather frightening to think that we are a similar age, as I can't wrap my arms around its trunk any more. I must be getting old.

With bulb-planting complete for the year, I turned my attention to the *Catalpa bignonioides* (Indian bean tree) close to where I'd been working. This stunning tree will be pollarded sometime between January and February. If left unpruned, this plant can reach over 10m in height. Don't let this put you off, though. It responds well to being pollarded and this will keep it to a manageable size and improve the quality and size of the foliage it produces. Now that we are in tree-planting season you would be wise to look into the pruning technique of a tree as well as its ultimate height. If a tree can be coppiced or pollarded there is no reason at all not to consider it as a specimen for a small garden.

Once home, my day was completed in fabulous autumnal style. I sat on the sofa with a bowl of homemade apple crumble made with windfall apples from the garden. Who could ask for more?

Friday 26th October

The yew hedges have been cut in the garden – this was a matter of urgency as they're best clipped before the frost arrives.

It's vital that the clippings are placed in a tump to rot down well away from livestock. A mouthful of yew could kill or harm sheep, cattle and horses. If you're planning a country garden, you must not use yew as a boundary hedge if it backs onto fields.

Yew is an impressive hedge that can be pruned hard, which means it's easy to regenerate old plants. It's a plant that grows much faster than it's given credit for, especially in Herefordshire. I would estimate that here it grows a foot a year.

I'm all in favour of the hedge in a country or city garden. They offer so much interest and create a home for insects and birds. They're the road network for wildlife as they travel from garden to garden and they offer wonderful protection to the plot from harsh winds. I can't even begin to imagine how dreadful the garden would be if it were surrounded by wooden fence panels – you know, the ones that look very smart for a year and then slowly lean in one direction or the other as if they are slightly inebriated. For me, a fence panel is simply a temporary solution as a boundary until the hedge has grown up past it. In this garden, plants used for hedging are numerous. From aucubas, field maples, box, beech, hornbeam, through to laurels, hollies and hawthorn, they all have their individual charm, and together keep me comfortably cushioned in this four-acre garden.

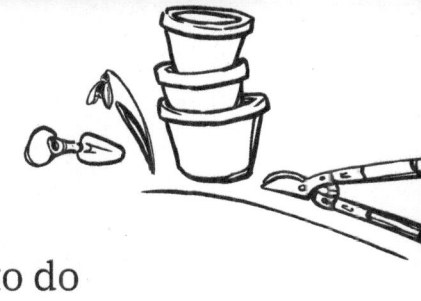

Things to do

- *Avoid locking the shed and retreating to the sofa: this is the month to take hold of the garden so take a week off work if you can.*

- *Visit an arboretum or woodland and admire the best of autumn.*

- *Make an apple crumble with windfalls – even an amateur cook can master this.*

- *Start or turn a compost heap.*

- *Move tender plants to a frost-free place and reduce the amount of water you give them.*

- *Remove shading from greenhouse and tunnels, and test out your greenhouse heater early in the month.*

- *Cut back summer-fruiting raspberries.*

- *Bring willow structures and wooden furniture undercover if you have room – they'll last longer.*

- *Plant trees, shrubs, hedges and perennials. Bare root plants are on sale now, and order roses for planting in winter.*

OCTOBER

Country Project

PLANTING TREES

You can buy a tree any time of the year, but wise souls will head to a specialist tree nursery this month when bare root plants are available.

I'm passionate about planting trees. A country garden without a tree just doesn't work for me – it's an essential ingredient. My great-great grandfather planted a monkey puzzle tree on the lawn at Stockton Bury in 1886 (or thereabouts) and it is still with us today. My uncle planted a tulip tree next to the monkey puzzle in 1976 and it's now vast. A visitor last year thought it was about 80 years old! Poor thing – they nearly doubled its age, and mine!

Trees should be planted for the future as well as the here and now. Put thought into which one will suit your family, your lifestyle and your growing environment. I like a tree that dances through the seasons in a different outfit each month. How about the striking *Malus transitoria*? It has incredible blossom, won't outgrow an average-sized garden and the flowers are followed by golden foliage and tiny orange crabapples that the birds will love. A tree is for life so give it plenty of thought and, in a few years, it will be the focal point of your garden.

Plant a tree in October or November and it will have the chance to set down strong roots and you should not have to water it in the heat of the summer, so you can book that trip to Spain after all! Plant two and you might even find yourself swinging in a hammock between them in a few years' time.

How to choose an apple tree

Not much beats an apple tree for a country garden. Cooker for crumble, or eating for crunch? Before you go shopping, write down your soil type, required height, aspect and how far the tree will be from a building and the experts will soon find the perfect match for you.

1. Make sure that you have a suitable pollinator nearby. Most apple trees need a pollinating partner - the apple tree in a neighbouring garden will do the job, or you can grow a self-fertile variety.

2. Choose the right rootstock. This controls the eventual height of your fruit tree. For some reason, rootstocks are named after motorways! M27 is very dwarfing (also my preferred route to Dorset), M9 is dwarfing, MM106 is semi-vigorous and M25 is the largest. There are a few other Ms inbetween, but you get my drift.

3. How do you want your apple tree to be trained – as a fan, standard, espalier or stepover? This will determine the position of your tree and some are more suitable than others for different types of training.

4. Bare root plants will be available this month, or you can get a container-grown tree later in the year. Buying bare root has many advantages: you can easily carry a 6ft tree without assistance, it's much cheaper, they settle quickly in the ground. And, of course, if packed carefully you can get an awful lot of plants into a car when the seats are down and then you won't need to vacuum the boot out!

Must-have plants

Anemone japonica
Clematis tangutica
(for seed heads)
Kniphofia rooperi
Chrysanthemums
Rosa glauca (for hips)
Rosa rugosa (for hips)
Hylotelephium (Herbstfreude Group)
Hesperantha coccinea
Skimmia japonica 'Rubella'

NOVEMBER

This garden is my free gym

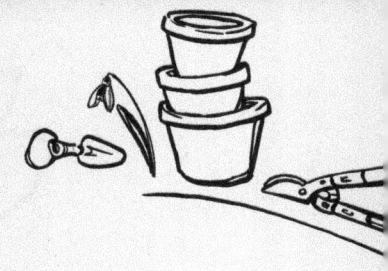

Tool Kit

Tree stakes and ties for your flock
of new woody plants.

Rabbit guards to protect new woody plants
from the nibblers.

Slippers with garden-proof bottoms –
ideal for those quick dashes outside.

A hairdryer! If you're not gardening at home,
take one to work. It's such a relief to be able
to dry your hair after getting soaked in icy
cold rain.

A deep wheelbarrow to collect
hedge clippings.

November

Not many things in life are certain but I'm confident that Jack Frost will arrive this month. The other certainty is that, for a short moment, I will consider finding a job that involves sitting at a desk in a warm centrally-heated office!

Tender plants are tucked up safe and the cattle are in the barns on beds of golden straw, but gardeners must face the weather. Without my sheepskin gilet and tights tucked into my knickers, I surely would not survive the winter.

Never has a year passed here at Stockton Bury without trees being planted in November. I estimate that in the last 20 years, well over 2,000 trees have been planted on the farm. Planting for future generations is an essential task this month and one that every country gardener and farmer should embrace, even if your plot won't stretch to thousands of saplings. With tree stakes and ties at the ready, it's time to dig deep and get to work. The excitement of planting a new tree never fades. Energetic tasks are to be embraced – they'll keep you warm.

… NOVEMBER …

Thursday 8th November

Where do gardeners go on holiday? Well, may I recommend where I have spent the last week – the "Island of Flowers", Madeira?

I have returned refreshed and with hands free of ingrained soil thanks to a daily dip in a (freezing cold) pool. I'm not a huge fan of houseplants, having spent a large part of my early horticultural life cleaning ficus and dieffenbachia leaves in Barclays International Bank in Poole. When you see them flourishing outside in Madeira you see their true glory. It almost seems criminal to leave them lurking in an office corner, starved of light and watered with coffee dregs.

I have returned to a naked tulip tree (every last leaf has fallen), a large pile of prunings and shorter days. My gardening day now ends at four o'clock due to low light levels and a desperate need for a bucket of hot tea. From now until spring I will be a 'barrow bitch'. My uncles are very good at leaving piles of prunings in the garden and I can't stand to leave the stems to blow about the garden. It's extremely tempting to use this irreverent title when writing my biography for a talk: RHS judge, ex-editor, currently Stockton Bury's barrow bitch! I'm quite content with my clearing-up role, however. Every time the uncles prune something, I learn from them. I shall never tire of watching them masterfully and confidently tackle a shrub – I hope one day I'll prune with such fearlessness and someone will clear up after me!

The piles of twigs to collect up on my return from holiday are those of the fig and the large mulberry tree. I have been trying to persuade my uncle to reduce the size of the mulberry for some time, as it had put on such impressive and energetic growth in the last few years. He had so far been loath to do so. "I love seeing the branches of trees sweeping the grass. In the fields the cattle and sheep always nibble off the lower branches," he explained.

I now fully understand his reasoning – it's a rather wonderful thought from the farmer-gardener. So, I was surprised on my return to see the lower branches had been removed. I'm thrilled – whether he is, it remains to be seen but at least I know he sometimes listens to me.

Raking continues: it's especially important to get the leaves off the lawn to prevent damaging it. This might seem a thankless task, but I've decided that the joy of gardening is not so much what you do but what you see whilst doing it. Rake in hand, and barrow by my side, I admired the birds, the seed heads and the last remaining hips on *Rosa moyesii* 'Geranium'. I'm also driven on by the thought that I'm improving my stomach muscles as I work – this garden is my free gym.

The latter part of the day was spent cutting back the herb bed. Disturbing the foliage released the scents of summer under a winter sky. Oregano, rosemary and sage filled the air.

On arriving home this evening, after a day in the garden being soaked by intermittent showers, a different sort of soaking was calling. Now that the nights have drawn in, I am destined to make a habit of my winter routine: light the woodburner, have a hot bath and spend the rest of the evening in my pyjamas. Country gardeners rarely head out for a night on the town – they're far too exhausted to bother.

Friday 9th November

Today it felt as if autumn was losing its grip and winter had the tighter hold. Grey skies covered the garden and the most uplifting colour was offered by the gold leaves of the silver birch.

My task was to clear up the yew clippings from the hedge that runs along the drive. This hedge caused a family dispute in the past. When my uncle planted it, over 30 years ago, my grandfather was so appalled that he pulled the curtains across the windows of the house. He was incensed that anyone could plant a poisonous yew hedge on a farm even if it was out of reach from farm animals. I wondered today whether he would have changed his view now that the hedge is so impressive. I clearly recall the arguments about this hedge around the Sunday dinner table. My uncle, planter of said hedge, is still terrified of the yew clippings ending up somewhere on the farm so they must be barrowed right to the other end of the garden – up and down steps! Barrow after barrow was pushed down the garden to ensure the yew's final resting place was well away from any and all livestock.

As a reward for clearing up a mountain of clippings, I headed to our local tree nursery (Frank P. Matthews) to eye up a few specimens. It's tree planting time and the perfect conditions to plant bare root hedging plants, raspberries and shrubs. Buying trees out of their pots is not only cheaper but they also tend to establish quickly and are light, so they're much easier to transport home. Nurserymen and women know their stuff and will help pair you up with the right tree so it's definitely worth heading to a specialist. The staff act very much like a dating agency. Give them a list of requirements and they'll find you the right match for life. Buying a tree should be taken as seriously as finding a life partner, however I'm sure it will be easier.

Thursday 15th November

It was incredibly mild today with temperatures hitting 12°C at midday. Colette and I set about pruning the hydrangeas.

NOVEMBER

We have a row of them at Stockton Bury running alongside the fruit frame. They offer shocking pink colour for most of the summer. To invigorate each plant, and to prevent them from drifting too far onto the sloping grass path in front of them, our pruning method is brutal. At least half of the old wood is cut right back to the ground. By doing this, the plant will put its energy into the newer stems, which will flower this coming summer. We quickly learnt that two people can't prune one plant. Coming at a plant from either side with sharp objects will only end in tears. You wouldn't be comfortable having two hairdressers clipping away at your barnet, would you? The result would be a wonky fringe at the very least. Pruning should take time, thought, and lots of stepping back and studying your subject.

Clearing up the clippings under the box hedging was our next task. If you leave the clippings lying around, you will increase the chance of your hedge being affected by box blight disease. The box hedging here is clipped once a year – cut it too often and the plants become compact and more susceptible to disease. May or October are the best months to clip box (we're running a little late this year!). In the border below the low box hedge, *Iris reticulata* is flowering. These summery-looking irises seem very out of place in the winter garden but it's a joy to have the blue and yellow flowers now. I also notice that the shoots of the perennial spring pea, *Lathyrus vernus*, are lurking just above the soil. If you look very closely at your plants at ground level, you'll understand how they grow so much better. For example, if you pull an old and faded rosebay willowherb, you'll notice that a new plant is forming at its base, just under the soil. This is a good reason to make sure you pull all of the weed and not just the top.

Today I admired the determination of two robins having a little dispute and found plenty of empty snail shells that had been neatly scooped out by hungry birds. As it is game-shooting season locally, we have a few rather smart male pheasants taking refuge in the garden. Nearly every year one or two seem to make the garden their home for months on end and we enjoy their regal presence. These handsome birds are most welcome to sprint and flutter about our borders.

The weather was so wonderful today that Colette and I sat by the pond to eat our lunch. We were joined by a few honeybees, which only goes to show how warm it was. A lovely habit that we've got into recently is to pick a gardening book to pore over during our break that might solve a question we've come up with during the morning. Today's book was *The Country Diary of an Edwardian Lady* by Edith Holden. First published in 1906 with the title *Nature Notes*, and containing details of each season, it was fascinating to see how Edith's notes of the month compared to our garden today. In November, Edith writes of admiring fungi – our fungi are over now and certainly beyond admiring. Could this be a sign of climate change or is it just the fact that we've had a wet autumn? As we read, my mother appeared and told us the rather sad tale of the author's death (there are very few books my mother hasn't read). It is thought that whilst walking by the River Thames near Kew, she leant over the water to reach a chestnut branch to admire it closer and fell into the river and drowned. How tragic. I hope after completing this diary I won't suffer such a fate!

The daylight hours have dwindled to such an extent that my gardening day is finished just before four o'clock. I can't say I'm sorry to down tools after a full day of trekking back and forth to the compost heap with barrow loads of leaves – when will it end?

Monday 19th November

The postman always leaves our letters in the garden shed at Stockton Bury and my uncle collects them almost immediately from the potting bench each morning.

Today the pile of post is still sitting there at 10 a.m. This means that something big has happened or is about to happen. My suspicions were confirmed when the vet's car pulled into the yard: he's here to do TB testing on the cattle on the farm. It's not just the stress of the results – Bovine Tuberculosis would be extremely serious – dealing with huge beasts is anxiety-provoking in itself. As my services have not been requested in the cattle yard, I'm making a sharp exit to the very far end of the garden to stay well out of the way. The vet will be back again on Thursday to see how the cattle have reacted to the injection. I can't even imagine how upsetting it will be if we have TB on the farm as this will lead to the slaughter of cattle to prevent it spreading.

 The bearded iris bed is nicely tucked away so it's here that I choose to spend the day. The bed in this sunny spot, just in front of the south-facing wall to the side of the fruit frame, has been full of irises for as long as I can recall. Although well placed, it is not well designed. Being about 6m long and about 2.5m wide, it is impossible to reach the centre of the bed without stepping into it. Stepping onto a bed packed with newly forming shoots of iris plants is not to be recommended. A word to the wise – if you're planning an iris bed, make it narrower unless you have incredibly long arms.

 As I was reminded today, if you leave tidying the iris bed until November, you can put your secateurs down. A quick tug will pull the faded foliage away, leaving behind the newly forming leaves for next year. If you race through iris with your snippers you are at risk of cutting off next year's shoots, which would be a disaster. You'd be wise to remove any weeds you spot at this time too, as the less you step in and out of the bed the better.

After seeing the vet's car disappear down the farm track, I decided I was safe to head out. My destination once again was the local tree nursery. On arrival, I quickly discovered that the two silver birch specimens selected were very unlikely to fit in the car. Not to be defeated, the back seats were flattened. The trick to travelling with trees is to put the head of the tree into the car first and the pot or bare root in last. After all, the top of a new tree is pretty flexible. Success! I used a few lengths of bailer twine to bind the top branches together in order to drive safely. What would we do without bailer twine?

Looking back at my plant-buying past, I must confess to having trees poking out of the sun roof on occasion. My most memorable journey was travelling a tree fern home in my soft-top MG. I had belted the tree into the passenger seat. On meeting my first set of lights I panicked when they started to change to red, so I jumped them to save the tree. The terrible letter with points arrived a few days later! All to save a plant from harm. I won't do that again.

Tuesday 20th November

Due to very bad planning, all of my gardening trousers have been washed at once and are currently too wet to wear.

With no other option, I delved into the bottom of my wardrobe to find the next garment to be downgraded to garden duty. My selection was a pair of high-waisted black jeans. I can report that this was a dreadful decision. They were far too tight and it was completely impossible to climb a gate – my gardening has been hindered all day. This pair is now garden-stained and only fit for a scarecrow, and a rather skinny one at that.

Sunday 25th November

By about 3.50pm the light is fading to such an extent that it's almost dangerous to keep working outside. Secretly, I quite like the fact that the afternoon cup of tea has been brought forward a little.

It's too cold to garden this week and a frosty morning is becoming normal. I'm also happy to escape the distinctive smell of rotting fruit. The cider apples have all been collected up and are now being transformed into cider at the local depot, but the remaining pile of rotting apples by the loading bay is rather pongy. In the garden, medlars are hanging ripe in the trees. Eaten raw they're dreadful, but when made into a jelly they are fit for a king. It's just unfortunate that these fruits bear such an unattractive common name: 'dog's arse'. Mind you, they do look like one.

Now that the temperature has dropped, it's the perfect time to work by the pond. The pond is very close to the beehives and, although I'm a brave girl, I don't see the point of working alongside busy bees. Today they are at rest. The plants around the pond are almost unrecognisable at this time of year. The only one that stands up with any glamour is the miscanthus at the back of the bed. Other than that, the aquatics in and around the water are slush. When working by a pond, don't work alone – we wouldn't want you to meet the same fate as Edith!

NOVEMBER

In the borders, the alstroemeria have sent up new shoots and the muscari bulbs I planted only a month ago have put on leaves. Things are still growing. It's with great excitement that the first snowdrops were spotted in flower today. Some here will flower as early as November and others will be with us until March. Of all the plants, it's the snowdrop that gives gardeners that feeling of being a plant hunter. We know we have them, of course, but their first appearance is always met with unexpected glee.

Things to do

- Forget about fireworks (no country-dweller should light them) and have a game of apple-bobbing instead – far more fun.

- Get the bones of your new garden in place now – by which I mean trees and hedging.

- Admire the show that naked trees bring. For polished bark grow Prunus serrula and for coppery peeling bark Acer griseum.

- Make friends with someone who owns a generously sized van, so you can borrow it when you go tree-shopping.

- Plant broad bean seed directly into the vegetable patch.

- Pick medlars and master the art of making jelly.

- Visit the garden centre but don't get starstruck by the Christmas baubles – now's a great time to buy roses and get planting.

- Continue to cut back faded perennials.

- Lift dahlias after they've been blackened by the first frost.

Country Project

MASTERING THE ART OF PRUNING

Approach pruning with confidence – don't be scared. After all, you own the plant so no one is likely to tell you off for a mistake.

Many of the trees and shrubs in the garden here at Stockton Bury are at their mature height. Nearly all the trees have had their lower branches removed at some point. Without doing this, the plants below would soon fade away or, in extreme cases, the tree would need to be taken out altogether. It's quite remarkable how many plants will appear in a shrubbery the year after a rather brutal pruning session. Snowdrops, eranthis and anemones that you'd forgotten about will suddenly show their faces thanks to an injection of light.

You'd be amazed how much woody growth is pruned out at this time of year in our garden. Without taking the matter in hand, you not only lose your underplanting but you end up with giant shrubs with a few flowers around the edges, and a bare network of stems in the centre taking up metres of your precious garden space. Pruning not only allows you to keep shrubs compact and productive but it also allows you to walk through the garden without being smacked in the face left, right and centre by branches.

There's so much to learn about when it comes to pruning so I'm not even going to attempt to explain it all, but I'm happy to share the greatest lesson I've learnt over the years: once you've cut it off you can't stick it back on!

Top tips for pruning success

Not much beats an apple tree for a country garden. Cooker for crumble, or eating for crunch? Before you go shopping, write down your soil type, required height, aspect and how far the tree will be from a building and the experts will soon find the perfect match for you.

1. Timing is everything. Some shrubs flower on old wood and others new. Look up your shrubs and make a list of what needs pruning when. You will rarely kill a plant by pruning it at the wrong time of year, but you will miss out on a year's worth of flowers.

2. Gather your tools. A decent pair of secateurs is vital, as is a small, folding pruning saw. I also find a pair of long-handled loppers handy on occasion. Using sharp tools and taking clean cuts will prevent the spread of disease (says the girl with no spring on her secateurs and plastic tape holding her folding saw together!).

3. Consider before you cut. Before you start wielding sharp blades, step back and make a plan. Look carefully at the plant and work out which branches to remove. Clever pruners will leave a shrub or tree in a neat shape, and remove crossing or rubbing branches. (Try to avoid clipping shrubs into lollipop shapes, though, as this really isn't a good look for a country garden – keep it natural.)

4. Be brave. If you fail to prune hard enough you will quickly lose a garden, ending up with massive shrubs with not much else growing underneath them. In a small plot this leads to disaster, but even if you have a larger garden you need to be mindful. Too much shade cast by shrubs and trees leads to a mossy lawn and a very dark and dingy plot.

Must-have plants

Chimonanthus praecox
Cornus mas
Cornus sanguinea 'Midwinter Fire'
Daphne bholua 'Jacqueline Postill'
Eranthis hyemalis
Euonymus oxyphyllus
Hamamelis
Iris unguicularis

DECEMBER

A pocket full of
mucky tissues

Tool Kit

Thick tights and thermal underwear.

Thin cotton gloves for double gloving.

Headband or woolly hat.

Plenty of hot water – after a day in a cold garden nothing warms you up like a hot bath.

A poinsettia, because Christmas isn't complete without one.

A basket to collect pine cones and seed heads to make into decorations.

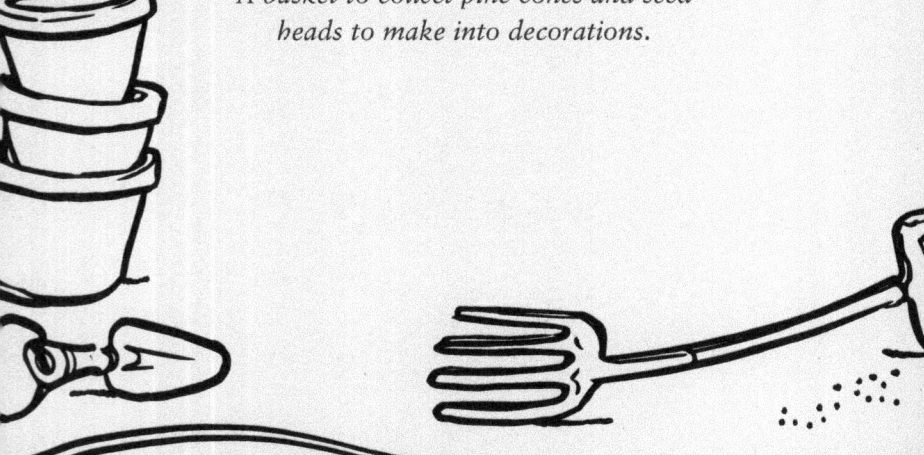

December

A country Christmas is all I know and I can't imagine being anywhere other than home to celebrate. You certainly won't find an artificial tree in my house. After all, what would life be like without clearing up needles well into June!

For the last six years or so I've been able to cut a Christmas tree from my mother's garden – planting a group of very small trees many years ago must have saved us a fortune. Their slightly mismatched shapes are all part of the charm.

In the garden and on the farm, it's time to remove dead and damaged branches from trees, and collect up fallen branches. These can be cut up into logs and stored for next year's firewood. Whilst most of the country is enjoying Christmas shopping, we will be dragging wood across muddy fields in our wellies. It's one garden task that my husband seems to adore – whatever the weather.

We haven't had a white Christmas here for years, which I'm sure the sheep on the farm appreciate. A dusting of frost is all I want for Christmas, so that the garden can simply sparkle.

DECEMBER

Saturday 1st December

Pinch, punch, first of the month.

Having just spent two days in London, I am quickly realising that we country folk are the last to be embraced by the Christmas spirit. The city was a feast of festive excitement and I came home feeling that we needed to jump on the bandwagon. Today I put my wreath that's decorated with pinecones on the front door and threw sparkling fairy lights around the kitchen. As I write, the constant flickering that bounces off my computer screen is starting to jar!

In the garden, most of the trees are bare but a few determined fruits cling to the branches of the apple trees. They are the best baubles that the season can offer. *Viburnum* x *bodnantense* 'Dawn' is filling the air with perfume. It's one of the first scented winter-flowering shrubs to perform. If planting a scented winter shrub, make sure you place it somewhere that you can enjoy its sweetness: by the front door, perhaps, near a seat or at the front of a border. It's no good if you have to climb through a border to take a sniff.

Mistletoe is in fine fettle here. Being only a few miles from Tenbury Wells (the acknowledged centre of the mistletoe universe) we have plenty. Although mistletoe is associated with Christmas it has been in berry since August in the garden. Few people in Herefordshire will be on the lookout for mistletoe – like an excess of apples, you can hardly give it away in this county.

It is surprisingly mild here (we still haven't put the heating on yet). Living in a rather old house that I refer to as 'The Colander' there seems little point putting the heating on anyway. There are a few advantages to having a cold house – flowers last for weeks indoors and my Christmas tree hardly drops a needle. It is at this time of year that I crave a full vase of flowers to enjoy throughout these dark evenings. Another quirk of the house, and a very poor mobile phone network, means that I do have to venture outside of an evening in the dark. The only place where I can receive a call is in the garden. Last night I chatted to a friend in the drizzling rain with the background music of owls hooting. How magical.

Friday 7th December

Now the borders are all cut back, it's time to get serious. Each bed needs to be gone through to remove perennial and annual weeds.

Hairy bittercress (*Cardamine hirsuta*) or 'Jumping jacks' as we like to call them, are popping up all over the place, so vigorously that you'd think we were at the height of spring. Groundsel (*Senecio vulgaris*) and rosebay willowherb (*Chamaenerion angustifolium*) are also unwelcome visitors, along with dandelions, of course. The mild weather has encouraged the weeds to remain the dominant force in the borders, so the more scratching around and searching for them that is done now the better. It really pays to be picky.

Colette and I are spending six and a half hours a day looking for weeds. If you have a companion in the garden, unlike many other workplaces, it is wholly acceptable to talk while you're working. The breadth of conversation is quite wonderful. Today we covered Brexit (of course), property, sexuality and health. In my opinion, a far better conversation can be had when kneeling in a shrubbery, whilst wearing a rather dashing bobble hat, than at any bar or dinner table. When your head is down, focusing on the weeds, you seldom make eye contact so you can talk to your heart's content without ever knowing that your companion is tiring of you! Speaking of bobble hats, Larry is in trouble. He's pulled the bobble off Colette's hat.

There are a few rather dashing surprises in the garden this month. If I were a plant, I'd choose to be one that offers winter interest. There are too many other beauties vying for attention in summer, but everyone is pleased to see a winter interest plant. The shocking purple berries of *Callicarpa bodinieri* var. *giraldii* 'Profusion' were certainly a joy today. I'd forgotten we had this plant and, on looking up the credentials of this deciduous shrub, I was reminded how easy and accommodating it is. It seems to have fallen out of fashion but I'm not sure why as it thrives in any aspect and almost any soil, and is a sure bet for winter colour.

After a late lunch, I decided to prune the rather unruly parthenocissus that climbs up and over a barn. It had made its way up into the guttering and under some roof tiles. I attempted to loosen its grasp last year but bottled out when the ladder started to sway. This year it cannot be ignored. There are many different types of parthenocissus and most of them are vigorous. Ours is *Parthenocissus quinquefolia*, which has the power to climb up to fifteen metres. These plants have little suckers that help them climb with gusto, so are not for the faint-hearted pruner. We have the space here to cope with such a romper but we still occasionally need to remind it who's boss. Grown for their incredible autumn colour, we admire the fiery red leaves as they tumble from the top to the bottom of the barn wall like a blood-red waterfall. To see the full potential of this climber, a trip to Hever Castle in Kent is the answer. The front of the castle is decorated from floor to turret with wonderful autumn foliage.

My efforts to control this handsome fellow started with cutting back the stems that grow away from the wall with secateurs. As I tackled the monster, I was quickly instructed by my uncle to use hedging shears. I ignored his advice, as I wanted one hand to hold onto the ladder – my uncle is obviously far braver than I am, even though Colette was at the foot of the ladder. Next I cut the stems that looked likely to be those that had grown up under the eaves. All that was left was to pull the stems and hope that they came away. Pulling plant growth from the top of a ladder is not something I would recommend. But, with a little more bravery than last year, I achieved my goal. If you're going to tackle a climber I'd suggest you do it in the morning. Mid to late afternoon in winter is not the best time to be up a ladder. Low winter sun can mean it's a job to see what the devil you are doing.

At dusk, I took a stroll down to the far end of the garden and was met on the top path by a rather jolly clump of *Iris reticulata*. This low-growing perennial offers a delicate scent – certainly a good reason to drop to your knees and smell it.

I spent my evening in a local village hall. No, not a gardening talk but bingo. With the world modernising at such a pace it is a relief to be down a country lane, in a hall with a tin roof. After a few rounds, I quickly realised that pastimes that don't give you time to talk to your companions are not for me – I'll stick to gardening. Bingo requires far too much concentration.

Thursday 13th December

Gosh, it's been cold today! So cold that it was time to double-glove. Colette has been astute enough to buy some thin cotton gloves from the pharmacist to wear under gardening gloves. This works a treat. I've also double-socked today.

My mother appeared dragging a large builder's ton sack into the garden. That could only mean one thing – she wants me to do something and that something is bound to be linked to the village church. Lo and behold, I was right. A large bag of holly and ivy was required to decorate for Christmas. It's hard for people to believe, but we really don't have spare clippings in the garden. We are so well pruned by this stage that straggly branches of holly are off the menu. In order to fill the sack, Colette and I headed out in the open-backed

DECEMBER

Land Rover but, afraid of getting stuck in muddy fields, I chickened out. We decided to clip the holly from my uncle's roadside hedges instead, leaving the wheels of his beloved Land Rover firmly on the tarmac. The downside to this is that any passing car assumes you are pilfering. With hazard lights blinking, we clipped berry-laden holly from the hedge and fled to the church quick smart. As I dragged the large sack up to the church porch, I congratulated myself for demonstrating goodwill to all men. Well, at least to the three women who will be decorating the church this year!

When the weather is this cold, you need to pick your task carefully. Raking leaves is an almost unbeatable way of warming up. As I cleared underneath the silver pear (*Pyrus salicifolia* 'Pendula') and the corkscrew hazel (*Corylus avellana* 'Contorta'), I spotted a robin on the wall. With bundles of mistletoe hanging from the trees over my head and a robin perched on the wall, I felt as if I was in a Christmas card.

It might be bitterly cold but alstroemerias have put on plenty of new shoots in the border as has the perennial everlasting pea, *Lathyrus rotundifolius*. In the vegetable garden, the broad beans that my uncle sows every year on his birthday, November 15th, are showing. Having removed the leaves of the hellebores, I can now clearly see the fat buds just appearing above the soil surface – how exciting. Last year's leaves are not required by the plant now and by removing them the plants are less susceptible to hellebore leaf spot disease.

My nose has not stopped running today and trying to wipe one's nose with a tissue when wearing muddy gloves is not easy. Why does your nose run even when you don't have a cold? Muddy tissues in gardeners' pockets are the norm. Speaking of coats, I've now got the perfect one. It's an army surplus camouflage coat that covers my bottom and has deep pockets. In those pockets are mucky tissues, dog treats, string, hair pins and chocolate. What else could a girl need?

DECEMBER

This evening I'm going to make Christmas decorations from items foraged from the garden. In my basket on the kitchen table are seed heads of sea hollies (eryngiums), pine cones, holly, ivy and the long whips of the wisteria. My plan is to use the wisteria stems to make hearts and circles to decorate. The kitchen counter is covered with newspaper, the kettle is whistling on the Aga and I'm all raring to go. I've definitely got the Christmas spirit now. I'm glad to be working with plants but in the comfort of my home after a chilly day.

Saturday 15th December

The polytunnel has been a hive of activity today, with the doors shut and the thermostat turned up. All that was missing was the dulcet tones of Christmas carols – after a couple of years of being kept in this sweaty tent the radio has given up. I suspect it is full of water.

The mission today was to put all the tender, evergreen agapanthus up on the staging. They started the winter on the ground but if the heater fails they won't cope with the cold, so up they go to give them a chance. After shuffling plants from here to there, I spent a little time removing the leaves from the tender geraniums. They are very susceptible to mildew, so picking them over will surely help. Whilst disposing of rotting leaves, I noticed that the *Cardiocrinum giganteum* (giant Himalayan lilies) in the pots at my feet had busily been producing babies over the summer. Cardiocrinums can take over ten years to flower from seed so I set to work removing the fat bulbs from their pots and carefully peeling away their babies to give them a life of their own. These impressive plants are monocarpic, so once they flower the bulb dies and more babies are produced to take over. There is little more satisfying than dividing plants such as this. Creating a second generation so quickly and easily is an opportunity not to be missed.

Friday 21st December

The weather remains kind to us – we haven't been knee-deep in snow or had any vicious frosts. I'm not a fan of a mild Christmas, though.

A mild winter gives plants a false sense of security and they enthusiastically start to shoot. The tulips in my containers are showing and the muscari I planted in October in small terracotta pots are positively vibrant with foliage, so I'm secretly hoping that the temperature drops just a little.

Today I've been clearing the leaves from the sunken garden. The school term has ended and my rather energetic son is eager for his mother to stand in a football goal. Gardening a couple of miles away from my home gives me a wonderful reason to escape! As I worked, I was joined by a robin hoping I'd unearth some tasty worms. This robin fooled me into thinking that I might just be able to reach out and touch him but he was as sharp as a knife and quick to manoeuvre away from my advances.

Our friendly beekeepers appeared today to look at their bees and it was a wonderful excuse to down tools and chat about the year that has passed. As we talked, I noticed one of them holding a brown paper bag. I found myself hoping that it contained their exquisite honey-coated nuts by way of a Christmas gift. There are so many benefits to having hives in the garden but these sugary nutty treats are by far my favourite. After our chat (and receiving a bulging bag of nuts and two lovely beeswax candles) I reflected on just how wonderful it is that, in this modern age of technology, two conveyers of very rural crafts can stand in a garden and talk for a generous amount of time about their year. I wonder if the conversation is that different to ones held centuries ago between a beekeeper and a gardener? The weather, when things flowered and what quantity of honey was drawn were surely just as relevant then as now.

Whilst I worked and chatted, my faithful Border terrier Larry spent his day sitting in the barrow wearing a rather dashing new coat. He has worked out that sitting in a nest of leaves is far warmer than choosing the cold grass. His lead is tied to the barrow; I only wish I could let him loose but being a terrier he'd be gone – goodness only knows what damage he would cause! He happily comes backwards and forwards to the compost heap with me and I'm sure that my uncle must often watch from the window as I try to push a loaded barrow through the garden without tripping over the lead and dog. I can almost hear the words "Stupid girl" every time I head for the compost heap. However, Larry is good company and seems very content to join me.

I left the garden today with a car boot full of mistletoe to decorate the house. We are literally drowning in it here. Uncle suggested only a few weeks ago that I should drive to London and try to sell it on a street corner. "Exactly which street corner would you like your niece to stand on?" was my reply. I'm pretty sure the last time he went to London he would have been driving a horse and carriage with Lord Byron for company! Joking aside, he might have a point – there must be a way to sell our amazing bounty. If I hang any more mistletoe around my door people will start avoiding a visit unless they are desperate for a kiss.

Monday 24th December

I adore Christmas Eve even more than Christmas Day.

A trip to the Regal Theatre in Tenbury Wells for the panto is followed by wrapping presents at the kitchen table, assisted by a large glass of ginger wine. If I can stay awake, Midnight Mass at the village church rounds the day off wonderfully. I'm the woman in the congregation who wears a Father Christmas hat, which is not embarrassing for my son at all!

As a family, we try our utmost to buy all our presents from our local market town, Leominster. We believe in local, but we're not big present buyers. For me, it's more about tucking into a giant Stilton (from the excellent local cheese shop The Mousetrap) and going on a long walk on the farm after Christmas dinner. Having said that, I must say I'm hoping for some alpaca socks and new secateurs.

Happy Christmas, everyone!

Saturday 29th December

To get out of lugging logs across a soaking wet field, I took a turn around the garden today. Listening to the droning of my husband's chainsaw in the distant orchard I admired the first hellebores, eranthis and witch hazel.

The snowdrops are shooting out of the ground and their white tips are just showing. These are all wonderful additions to the winter garden but I'm yearning for a dusting of frost. No one wants an early spring. I even spotted a honeybee feeding on a hellebore – now that will give the beekeepers and I something to talk about when I next see them in the New Year.

Things to do

- *Harvest and make your own Christmas decorations from the garden.*

- *Prune climbing roses and use some of the prunings to take hardwood cuttings.*

- *Plant tulips. It's not too late and they're better in the ground than sitting in the shed.*

- *Dig over the vegetable patch on a mild day. That'll shift a few excess Christmas calories.*

- *Brush snow off hedges and greenhouses, if it's a white Christmas.*

- *Get ahead now and have your mower serviced before spring.*

- *Cut up or shred prunings and add some much needed roughage to the compost heap.*

- *Continue to collect fallen leaves.*

- *Insulate your outdoor taps.*

DECEMBER

Country Project

A HOMEMADE COUNTRY CHRISTMAS

It's the most wonderful time of the year and it doesn't have to cost a fortune. By making your own decorations the children will really get a feel for the season and the excitement the winter garden offers.

My family are a frugal lot at Christmas. We feast mainly on one giant block of Stilton, a baked ham, turkey and plenty of jacket potatoes. The glitz is added to the table by jellies and jams that have been created from produce from the garden. Homemade kiwi jam on toast on Christmas morning, and lashings of crab apple jelly with the Christmas turkey are just some of the glistening delights on offer.

As for decorations, apart from a few baubles from the 1970s, the house is decorated with holly, mistletoe and ivy. I love collecting pine cones and seed heads from the garden to spray with silver and gold paint to add to the glamour. Dried hydrangea and eryngium flower heads are the best subjects for colouring up. You really can create a festive scene without spending a fortune on man-made decorations.

As the rooms are so cold in my house, a table centre of a potted hellebore is sheer perfection and there's always a bowl of hyacinths filling the room with their overwhelming scent. I'm a sucker for a real tree and we've always grown our own. They're not always perfect in shape but the fact that you've watched it grow is enough to make you fall in love with your tree whatever its weird and wonderful form. With a varied garden and a little bit of imagination you really can 'pick' your own Christmas.

How to make a Christmas wreath

1. Head out to the garden armed with a basket and secateurs. You're looking for berries, evergreen foliage, faded flowers of the hydrangea, cones, twigs and attractive seed heads. If you see any, pull sheeps wool off barbed wire fences and collect any feathers.
2. Either make your own wreath base from silver birch twigs bound together with florist wire or cheat and buy one (I won't tell anyone). The wire around the base will be handy to push your natural decorations under to hold them in place.
3. Using a piece of brightly coloured ribbon, make a loop around the top of the wreath frame so it can be hung from the door.
4. Start by wiring on the evergreen foliage to create a base and then add your natural decorations. The tricky bit is trying to hide the wire.

Must-have plants

Galanthus elwesii (my favourite snowdrop for its simplicity)
Garrya elliptica (for catkins)
Hellebores
Iris reticulata
Jasminum nudiflorum
Lonicera fragrantissima
Prunus serrula (for bark)
Rubus cockburnianus
Sarcococca hookeriana var. digyna

JANUARY

I don't hold my drink well at all

Tool Kit

A waterproof radio.

Wooden pallets.

Snowdrop identification book.

A snow shovel.

Sweet pea seed.

*Thick leather gloves,
for pruning gooseberries.*

*Disposable gloves and a good
set of paint brushes.*

January

With the excitement of Christmas over, there's a sense of relief, but this can be a very bleak month. The weather is always a concern – looking back at my old gardening diaries, anything can happen.

It's a time to leave the car in the drive, as narrow country lanes can be treacherous. I have been known to walk the four miles to Stockton Bury from home, pulling a sledge so I can whizz down the hilly bits. Farmers tend to stay put – what's new? – to be on hand to clear snow for drivers and ward off burst pipes on the farm (their biggest fear).

This is the month that I put my camera to best use. Every day I hope to capture the perfect shot of the garden glistening in frost before anyone steps foot on the grass. Speaking of grass – stay off it. Walking across a frosty lawn can leave more than a trail of temporary footprints, if the grass gets damaged.

We've had our foot on the throttle of the wheelbarrow since October so I can relax a bit now. Every January, when it's too cold to do much else, I paint. Benches, chairs, doors – you name it, I paint it. This always seems like a great way to while away a freezing cold day but the problem is that when it's very chilly, paint just doesn't dry. I know this fact well, but every January I seem programmed to rub down the woodwork and crack out the brushes. It serves me right that for most of this month I'll have hands, face and arms splashed with paint.

JANUARY

Tuesday 1st January

It might be the first day of the calendar year but for me the new gardening year doesn't start for a couple of weeks yet – I'm still on a bit of a go-slow after Christmas.

However, on a morning stroll around the garden with my camera I spotted plenty of signs of life. The galanthophiles I'm acquainted with are estimating that this year snowdrops are a fortnight ahead of time. The first of the eranthis have appeared and, at the foot of the south-facing kitchen garden wall, the impressive clump of Iris reticulata continues to flower. As I head deeper into the garden, I spot the witch hazel. It's far from fully out but definitely worth creeping into the border for a smell. It's mild today and I always think that the scent of winter shrubs is stronger on a cold day.

Today I'm thankful for all our hard work done before Christmas. Imagine if we hadn't cut back our borders yet? I would be unable to admire the sharp, enthusiastic spears of new growth from the snowdrops. The most exciting discovery today is spotting the Adonis vernalis – what an incredible name to give a plant! This low-growing poisonous plant has stunning bright yellow flowers. Why it was given the name of Adonis I'm not sure, but the dictionary definition reads 'a very beautiful or sexually attractive young man.' As a result, it's a plant name I never forget.

My walk concluded at the polytunnel, and as I approached I heard the roar of the oil-fired heater (it must be cold). Heating this giant monster isn't cheap. Very few people consider the hidden costs when purchasing a plant from a specialist nursery. "Oh, that's expensive," they say, but some of those plants will have spent four or more years growing in heated conditions over winter until they're ready to sell.

Saturday 5th January

My mother came back from the local library today with a basket of books to tuck into. On the top of the pile I spotted The Diary of a Farmer's Wife 1796–97 by Anne Hughes.

Anne's farm was in Herefordshire. Precisely where in the county no one really knows but, eager to find out more, I removed the book from the basket.

As I read under the light of my new Christmas head-torch (a great gift, as the lighting in my old house is rather dim) I was intrigued by daily life on a farm all those years ago and thrilled to see that, like me, Anne had started her diary at the beginning of February. Now life is changing fast and so many of the tasks carried out by my late grandmother are no more. I can just about remember her making butter in the dairy and that there was always a large bucket of warm milk on the kitchen table covered with a muslin. My grandmother would also wash clothes against a washing board in the sink, and almost everything was composted – including the best silver teaspoons and her wedding ring, discovered again by my uncle many years later when he created the garden!

On 14th April 1796, Anne writes of turning the lamb's tails that had been removed into a stew. Thankfully this is no longer on our menu. Great progress has also since been made in beekeeping. Before the modern beehive was invented, bees would settle in straw skeps. In order to remove the honey from the skeps, sulphur would be burned to kill the bees A big hole was dug for each skep before the sulphur papers were lit. Anne was clearly not a fan; she wrote of this activity as "such a waste of good bees".

Cider was a huge part of life on farms in Herefordshire in 1796. We still have a cider press at Stockton Bury and acres of orchards to go with it. Interestingly, the cider apples were picked on September 5th in Anne's diary; we leave ours until the beginning of October. Cider was served with almost every meal and seemed to be the perfect way to console a farmer who was mourning the loss of a cow. Tea was only for the very refined. This got me to thinking that the majority of gardeners and farmhands must have spent most of their adult working life a little pickled. Thank goodness for tea, as I don't hold my drink well at all!

The best entry is the mention of a homemade cure for scour (diarrhoea in cattle). A drench was made of crushed peppercorns and ginger, mixed with some 'pudding flour' and gin. Life in the country has certainly moved on but whether it has improved for the better I'm unsure. I don't expect that the verges beside the roads were littered then with old sofas and empty energy drink bottles. What would Anne say about that?

Friday 11th January

The last time I went to the cattle market I was a child. I was accompanying my grandfather all those years ago.

I clearly remember him giving me and my sister a bottle of Coca-Cola to drink on the journey. When we pulled into the market, he braked sharply and the cola shot out of our noses and covered the dashboard! He wasn't best pleased.

Today I joined my uncle as he went to sell his cattle. As soon as we arrived it became evident that, yet again, I was wearing the wrong thing. Everyone else was in a boiler suit, waxed coat and wellies and there were no other colours on offer apart from green and brown. I was resplendent in a bright blue jacket with velvet purple jeans and suede boots. I successfully stood out like a sore thumb – what was I thinking? When will I learn?

Our first port of call was the café. Bacon, egg and sausage baps were up for grabs. It quickly became clear that this was not just a place of breakfast and business for the farmers but, in some cases, much needed human contact. Many of them work alone in remote places so a bacon roll with a fellow farmer is the highlight of their month. My uncle and I were joined by a farmer from the Welsh hills at our table. He spat his bread at me as he chatted about the weather. Out of politeness, I sat and took the spit as I cradled my polystyrene cup. After all, I was the girl who spurted Coca-Cola out of my nose in this very place. When he left the table another farmer took his place and he and my uncle shared stories of their late fathers. Everyone knows everyone at the market and has done for decades. Not much had changed here in the last 25 years – apart from a woman arriving in purple velvet jeans!

Inside the market, the auctioneer was nothing short of impressive. Goodness only knows what he was saying. I was completely baffled, but the farmers were not. Cattle were sold at speed and the process was slick. You'll be pleased to hear that I kept my hands in my pockets and wasn't tempted to come home with a Hereford bull. On a cold day, this trip was a welcome break from clearing leaves.

Thursday 17th January

After recently writing a feature for a magazine on whether or not to pre-germinate sweet peas, I started the day by doing my own little experiment.

I had discovered during my research that some gardeners sow sweet pea seed direct, others soak them in water, some leave them for 24 hours on damp kitchen towels, and then there are those that chip them (nicking the seed coat with a knife). My experiment involved placing a few sweet pea seeds on damp kitchen roll in a sealed box, and planting some others straight away. In a few weeks' time I'll know which method worked the best for me. I suspect that the truth is there is no right or wrong way, but if you want to absolutely ensure that the seed you are sowing is viable it's a good idea to pre-germinate. However, if you are sowing hundreds of seeds time will probably not allow you to go through this process. (On the subject of sweet peas, I tend to prefer to sow them in November, as this gives stronger plants that will cope well if the summer is short on rain. But it never hurts to sow a few more in January, as then you'll get some later flowers to extend the scented show.)

The rest of my day was spent in the polytunnel repotting perennials that will be sold in spring and summer. Keeping a working nursery area of a garden tidy is almost impossible. Every winter I have the idea that I will organise it but it would be a huge undertaking, as throughout the year the plants are constantly being moved from sun to shade or inside and outside the polytunnel. The best we can hope to achieve is to repot everything, clear the leaves and use a hoe to scrape the lichen off the black matting that covers the floor.

All this activity would be made much more interesting if the radio worked. For a few moments it did make a gargling sound but it's so full of water now that I might need to throw Jeremy Vine and Zoe Ball a life raft. I should have put a new radio on my Christmas list.

Thursday 24th January

Yes, it's cold but the ground isn't frozen so great things have been achieved in the garden today. I've been pestering my uncle for a place to make leafmould for months and today he unveiled his pallet leaf store.

JANUARY

Who would have thought that four pallets held together by bailing twine would make a girl so happy? It looks just like a compost heap, but I was so excited by the new addition I started the day by clearing yet more leaves and enthusiastically piling them into the frame. Give it about eighteen months and I'll be happily spreading my own homemade leafmould on the borders. It's the best free soil improver on the planet.

Now that the borders are cut back and clear it's a good time to make a note of areas in the garden that need improvement. There is a bed under a thuja hedge that is hopeless. Even Verbena bonariensis hasn't made it here and that grows almost anywhere. It's just too dry. The only plant that seems to cope is an unknown ornamental grass so I decide that the solution is to make this a bed of grasses. Surely that will be a success? It's currently full of the dreaded couchgrass, a weed that seems deliriously happy there.

Another border that needs attention is the one by the swimming pool. Yes, we have a swimming pool and no, I don't use it very often. It's bloody freezing all year! Swimming pools are a lot of work to keep but my uncles brave the cold often in the summer, especially after a day of harvesting. They are obviously far hardier than me. Perhaps I have been eternally scarred by a teenage incident that revolved around this pool. I dived in and my new bikini came right off – in front of four boys from the village! I vividly remember running across the main lawn with only a lilo to hide behind.

The bed I refer to is south-facing yet shaded by the glass shelter that covers the pool. It's a real hot spot and a place where unusual plants such as Buddleja colvilei, Colutea arborescens and Colquhounia coccinea thrive. It's also home to hundreds of nerines. There are so many that you can see the bulbs pushing each other up above the soil surface. It's time for some of them to be moved. Colette and I lifted two barrowloads and wheeled them to their new home at the other end of the garden. They are now living at the foot of the wall of the alpine house in a south-facing spot and will be used as cut flowers in October when the garden has closed. When lifting and dividing bulbs I always feel as if I've won the lottery. It's as if you've found gold coins in the garden. We'll have to wait a couple of years before we can pick the nerines as they take a while to settle after being moved.

This chilly January day ended with myself, Colette and my two uncles sheltering from light drizzle in the alpine house. Two of us were cradling cups of tea and admiring the hepaticas and the other two (my uncles) were having a mini argument about potatoes. For the first time in my living memory they had had to buy potatoes from a shop – yes, a shop! One uncle wasn't at all pleased about this situation as we still had some in stores, but the other proclaimed that the very hot summer had caused our stored potatoes to develop an unsavoury taste. Potatoes are a serious issue for country folk. I chose not to get involved.

Saturday 26th January

There's been a flurry of snow today but nothing that will stop me from spending the day in the nursery area. Outside the polytunnel, the hardy perennials are left to cope with all weathers.

This might seem cruel when we have the space under cover but if you buy from a nursery that treats their stock mean you can be sure that the plants will cope well in most gardens. It's a little like asking someone who rarely steps out of their centrally heated home to trek across the Brecon Beacons – they just won't be

JANUARY

prepared and will be likely to fail. Tough love is what I believe in when it comes to plants. In early April, I'll quite often hear people rejoicing in this way: "Oh, Jean, you'll never believe it. I bought an alstroemeria and an osteospermum in full flower last week!" Well, Jean might well be impressed but most experienced gardeners will realise that plants in flower well before their time have probably been grown in a rather cushty heated polytunnel. Once planted outside they will go into shock and the flowers will be no more.

The space inside our polytunnel is reserved for tender plants such as Beschorneria yuccoides, bomarias, agapanthus and cardiocrinums. It's also home to the potting bench. Every single plant in the nursery area is repotted every winter with fresh compost with a slow-release feed mixed in. This is a rather daunting task that takes an age but it's vital for the plants' success.

Tucked behind an unruly row of Crocosmia 'Lucifer' I came across a rather handsome tray of Eurybia x herveyi. A handy plant, as it grows in full sun or part shade and thrives here in our clay soil. This perennial was once known as an aster but has been reclassified. It produces a profusion of pale blue daisy flowers in late summer. With only a few in the tray, the temptation to divide them was too much.

Once turned out of their pots it became obvious that they were virile and raring to grow. It's usually wise to leave the division of asters until early spring, as by then they will have recovered from putting all their energy into producing late summer and autumn flowers. By spring they will be ready to put on new roots and form impressive plants. As I pushed my old carving knife through the heart of the plant I wondered if late January could be classed as spring? Too late – my enthusiasm would not be dampened.

The garden is looking sharp with its beds cleared. I'm happy to see the bare soil as it allows those plants that do dare to shine in the cold an undisturbed backdrop. Snowdrops are in full bloom, eranthis is displaying flowers of yolk yellow and the perfume from winter shrubs such as Cornus mas, daphnes and witch hazel continue to fill the air with scent. We worked out today that the largest witch hazel at Stockton Bury is 52 years old. Uncle clearly recalls planting it – a fine example of how gardeners have incredible patience.

Thursday 31st January

I'm rather sad to have reached the end of this diary year. I've enjoyed wittering on to you about my adventures. What better way to end than with a celebration?

Today I attended a gathering of galanthophiles at Colesbourne Park in Gloucestershire. To be part of such an event is an honour indeed, as Colesbourne is one of the most important snowdrop gardens in the country. The snowdrop world is one of mystery, intrigue and incredibly knowledgeable people. Those from outside the circle should be on their guard and never try to guess a plant name – you'll quickly be caught out. Today I met people whose relatives discovered important snowdrops and I mingled with collectors who have paid hundreds of pounds for one bulb. Why are these tiny plants of such importance? I suspect it is because they are strong, beautiful and spread their love wherever they are seen.

After returning home, I walked the fields on the farm to collect wood. Two birds of prey were circling over an old oak tree that had sadly fallen. It was as if these birds were mourning its death with a respectful fly-past.

I am writing this final entry on a cold, dark January night. I can feel the creeping draught at my ankles that finds its way under

JANUARY

my back door. The dog is snoring and lying far too close to the woodburner. Life in the country might not always be comfortable, but it is rarely dull. I certainly feel at one with nature and I hope that I've managed to share the excitements and adventures that each season brings.

I'm not going to finish this book with a to-do list – if you've followed my advice so far, you'll have time to put your feet up before the warmth of spring starts the cycle all over again. One thing's for sure – before you know it you'll be running across the lawn barefoot and admiring the summer flowers. Until then, keep your top tucked into your pants and enjoy everything that winter has to offer.

JANUARY

Country Project

WELCOMING GARDEN BIRDS

If you've chosen to snuggle up inside this month, spare a thought for the garden birds. The weather is harsh and our feathered friends could do with some extra food to see them through the winter.

A richly planted country garden should provide a varied diet for visiting birds. However, offering birds additional food is very important in the colder months. They will repay you for your efforts by offering a daily scene of drama and romance with a backing track of bird song. What could be better?

Birds by their very nature are flighty creatures, so the best gardens are those that offer peace, quiet and safety. Gardens with generous plantings of trees and shrubs are more likely to see a wider range of visitors than those that are very open. A mixed hedge of blackthorn, hawthorn and holly is a certain way of pulling in the birds. If you offer bird tables, feeders and bird baths, ensure they are placed in an open spot to keep them safe from pouncing cats.

It's in January that I most regularly garden alongside a robin. As soon as I turn the soil, he swoops down and retrieves a worm. Robins are very territorial, so I can be almost sure that it's the same robin I'm talking to every day. (Yes, I do confess to having conversations with birds but I'm convinced the robin is taking it all in!) To treat him, I often buy mealworms, his favourite feast.

JANUARY

Top tips for bird lovers

1. To attract a wide range of birds it's worth researching what your favourite birds like to eat and how they prefer to be presented with their feast. Some prefer hanging feeders and others such as blackbirds, starlings and chaffinches prefer to eat from the ground. There's a wonderful selection of specialist bird foods available designed to attract different birds but you can also offer them suitable fresh kitchen scraps (fruit, dry cheese and fruit cake). Leave a few apples on the lawn for ground feeders.
2. Bird baths are just as important as bird tables – if not more so. What do you need after eating a bag of sunflower seeds or nuts? A drink, of course! The same applies to birds.
3. Keep bird tables and bird baths clean, and remove uneaten food regularly to prevent the spread of disease. I find cleaning a bird bath gives a great sense of satisfaction!
4. Last but most importantly, remember that once you start feeding birds, you must not suddenly stop as they will come to rely on you. In winter, they need all the help they can get.

SEASONAL TREATS

October

This is the month of stews and dumplings as the temperatures drop. Pork and cider casserole is a favourite in my household. After a day of vigorous leaf clearing, I'm starving as the light fades in the garden. I eat more this month than in any other but feel confident that I can work it off. You'd be wise to lift some of your carrots and store them in a frost-free dark place. I place them in an old wheelbarrow, cover with a damp towel and put them in the cellar (this will keep them fresh for a couple of weeks). Forage for elderflower berries, the last of the blackberries and pick the apples and pears. Save some berries for the birds, though. Don't forget to harvest those pumpkins for Halloween – leave them to get hit by frost and they'll turn to mush. Now that would be scary.

November

If there's been a very hard frost the parsnips will taste all the better for it, so wait until this happens before lifting them. Roast them or make a hearty soup. Parsnips are packed with fibre and are praised for lowering blood pressure – the perfect antidote to the stress of endless leaf clearing! It's not just parsnips that are good for your health - this month it's certainly possible to eat an apple a day to keep the doctor away. My advice is to avoid filling your fruit bowl. Keep your apples in a cool place instead, and when you pop out to get your snack take a few minutes to pick over the stored apples and remove any rotten fruits. The bruised apples can be put on the lawn for ground-feeding birds. I head to the cellar for my fruity snack wearing a head torch – anyone would think I was going mining for treasure. Well, I suppose in some way I am.

December

Brussels sprouts are ready to pick and made all the better after a hard frost. If you plan well, you can be eating cabbages or something that resembles a cabbage for the next four weeks. I expect that there will be many members of the family that will dread this prospect, but not me. I'm often asked if it is possible to grow your own Christmas dinner? It is, but careful storage of produce and a year of planning plays a huge part. Thanks to our cellar we have our own sprouts, potatoes, parsnips, carrots and leeks. Thyme and sage for the stuffing is picked from the garden on the day – this is a great job for children on Christmas morning (well, my mother always thought so). Round off a winter evening by cracking a few nuts by the fire. My hearth is usually home to a collection of shells by the time we all head off to bed. Hazelnuts are my favourite.

January

Leeks, spinach, Brussels sprouts and cabbage will ensure that no one is low in iron this month. You'll be relieved that you bothered to freeze fruit from the summer and autumn this month. A damson crumble is a warming and welcome treat. My grandmother used to have china bowls with flat lips around them and my sisters and I would line up the pips from the damsons around the edge of the bowl. We would recite the rhyme 'Tinker, Tailor' as we counted our pips. 'Tinker, tailor, soldier, sailor, rich man, poor man, beggar man, thief.' You might be entertained to know that none of us managed to marry a rich man!

Acknowledgements

Thank you to my supportive family and friends, especially my mother who never fails to display enthusiasm for anything I do. Also, to my husband Victor and son Herbie who try hard to pretend to be interested in my passion for horticulture!

I'd like to thank my uncles for allowing me to share their garden, Julian Stevenson for manoeuvring tractor and trailer into tight corners of the garden; Julian Hayes for arriving like a knight in shining armour in winter to help cut back the garden, Jim and Ryan Collett for cutting the lawns immaculately and Des Hall for building features in the garden. Thanks go out to Colette for her great company and help in the borders and to Louise and Nick from Seggin Bees for adding such a buzz to the garden. Oh, and I mustn't forget the amazing team in our garden café who keep me supplied with cake and our wonderful visitors who bring the garden to life in summer.

Lastly to Helen Bowden of Orphans Publishing who encouraged me to write this book, and to Hannah Madden and Rosalie Herrera for their beautiful illustrations.